C.S.
Lewis

WOMEN OF FAITH SERIES

Amy Carmichael
Corrie ten Boom
Florence Nightingale
Gladys Aylward
Hannah Whitall Smith
Isobel Kuhn
Mary Slessor
Joni

MEN OF FAITH SERIES

Borden of Yale
Brother Andrew
C. S. Lewis
Charles Finney
Charles Spurgeon
Eric Liddell
George Muller
Hudson Taylor
Jim Elliot
Jonathan Goforth
John Hyde
John Wesley
Martin Luther
Samuel Morris
Terry Waite
William Carey
William Booth
D. L. Moody

John and Betty Stam

C. S. Lewis

Catherine Swift

BETHANY HOUSE PUBLISHERS
MINNEAPOLIS, MINNESOTA 55438
A Division of Bethany Fellowship, Inc.

C. S. Lewis
Catherine M. Swift

Library of Congress Catalog Card Number 89-82261

ISBN 1-55661-126-9

Originally published by Marshall Morgan and Scott
Publications Ltd

Published by Bethany House Publishers
A Ministry of Bethany Fellowship, Inc.
6820 Auto Club Road, Minneapolis, Minnesota 55438

Printed in the United States of America

Contents

1

The Magic Lands of Boxon and Little Lea

C live Staples Lewis was born in Belfast, Northern Ireland, on November 28, 1898, just three and a half years after his brother Warren Hamilton. From infancy he and Warren were devoted to each other. As Clive said years later, "Our relationship was more than a close sibling companionship—in many ways we were confederates."

Their parents were cultured, intellectual, and physically attractive. Flora, their mother, came from a long line of lawyers, seafarers, and clergymen. She had attended Queen's University in Belfast, gaining degrees in mathematics, geometry, and algebra.

Their father, Albert Lewis, was a prosperous

solicitor who came from Welsh farming stock, but was born in Belfast after his father, Richard, moved to Ireland to take up engineering.

The couple met when Albert returned from Lurgan College to his parents' home to discover that the new vicar at the local church, Flora's father, was also their new neighbor. The Hamiltons and Lewises had already become firm friends when Albert and Flora fell in love, so their families were delighted.

Flora was a loving, serene, yet cheerful woman. On the other hand, Albert was extremely pessimistic, irritable, and prone to melodramatic outbursts. His life was so orderly, one could set a clock by him. Rich though the family was, he constantly predicted that they were heading for the workhouse. Nevertheless he was always generous, even affectionate in his own peculiar way. At times he was quite humorous, and his sons even claimed he was the best storyteller in the world as he always acted out the characters parts.

Their semi-detached home, Dundela Villa, was situated on the outskirts of the city, and from their bedroom windows the boys spent hours gazing out over the lush, green countryside towards the distant Castlereigh Hills—hills that seemed like another country compared to the hustle and bustle of Belfast's busy streets.

The boys' earliest years were enriched by an

abundance of love and fun from their nurse, Lizzie Endicott. But she, like Albert, was another human paradox, for although she was a down-to-earth countrywoman with loads of common sense, her mind was steeped in the romance of Irish folklore and legend. How her two small charges loved to snuggle up to her on cold, dark nights to hear stories of leprechauns and giants, of mythical beasts and gallant knights rescuing damsels in distress.

Their early years were also very normal for their middle-class background, with lessons from Miss Harper, a rather ordinary but kindly governess. They enjoyed month-long holidays at the seaside, trips to France, and visited neighbors and relatives living nearby. Reciprocal visits by neighbors and relatives at their house, however, were usually dreaded.

Whenever Flora and Albert had guests, their two small sons were expected to sit quietly in the drawing room listening to the boring conversation going on around them—boring to such young ears because invariably the subjects included politics and illnesses with an occasional reference to religion. Thus, Clive concluded that "grownup talk" meant those three topics, and though he wasn't enamored by talk about ailments or religion, he especially disliked the political discussions. Long before he even knew what politics was, he'd acquired a very jaundiced view of it.

Despite the occasional grownup talk about religion, Warren and Clive were given very little religious education. They were told to believe in God, to say their prayers nightly, and were regularly taken to church because "it was the right thing to do." But no one ever bothered to explain why.

Possibly even more unusual was their ignorance of beauty and art. They were surrounded by cultured family and friends, yet were never introduced to poetry. Flora didn't care for it and Albert was too concerned with the prospect of financial ruin and his organized routine to waste time on such unimportant matters. Everything about the couple seemed purely functional.

The large garden in which the boys played was seen as a whole, without regard for individual flowers, leaves, or trees. Clive's first awakening to anything remotely beautiful was when Warren made what he called a toy garden on an old cookie-tin lid. On a bed of sweet-scented moss he had piled up small twigs to resemble trees and used florets from bigger blooms to make flower borders. Clive was so taken aback at the perfect miniature form, the glistening dew and the fragrance, that he felt a sudden upsurge of emotion so powerful it could only be described as *Joy*—with a capital *J*.

His second encounter with Joy was when he discovered Beatrix Potter's animal stories, which he adored—especially those of Squirrel Nutkin. For hours he would sit gazing at the pictures, longing to gather hazelnuts on the island with Nutkin and Twinkleberry and to run around in the green and golden woods.

When he was five, and his brother eight, they began to write stories. Because of Beatrix Potter, Clive naturally involved animals but, as he also loved Lizzie Endicott's accounts of medieval chivalry, he combined the two. Then, wanting his stories to have a "grown-up" theme, he thought he'd better include "politics." So, in his "Animal Land," during the autumn, mice in medieval armor rode out on rabbit-back to fight battles with ferocious cats.

Being three years Clive's senior, Warren wrote stories that were more sophisticated. They took place in and around India, and were mostly about tall sailing ships and railway trains. To bring their stories together Clive and Warren compromised. Clive's mice sailed on ships and rode on trains, and Warren lifted India from the Asian continent and made it into an island next to Animal Land to form the "Boxon" nation.

In 1905, when he was six, a great upheaval took place in Clive's life. As was then customary in the middle-classes at the age of ten, Warren was sent away to boarding school in Hertfordshire, England. The brothers were terribly upset at being parted although they knew Warren would be home on holidays.

Meanwhile, Jacksie—Clive took an intense dislike to his name and demanded to be known as Jacksie—and his parents were moving into "Little Lea," an enormous new house much further from the city and a full twenty-minute walk to the nearest train stop. For variety it was ideally situated, backing on to open country while overlooking wide meadows that swept down to Belfast Lough, with its busy shipping always providing interest and excitement.

Perhaps moving just as Warren was leaving was good timing because it meant Jacksie also had a new experience ahead of him. To adults, Little Lea was possibly the worst designed house imaginable, to a child it was a world of mystery and adventure. The sanitation was disastrous, with every pipe in the house gurgling, hissing, and whooshing by day and by night. On the mildest day, a slight breeze was magnified to that of gale force as it whined and whistled through the rafters, rafters which also echoed every soft footstep and whisper.

Almost as if the builder had ordered too much material and didn't know how to dispose of it, the upper stories held several absolutely useless rooms, closets and attics of all shapes and sizes. And, as the new house could have no rusting nails, old splintered wood, or dirty areas where he could come to harm, Jacksie was permitted to explore to his heart's content.

To his amazement, no matter where he looked, there were books. Albert and Flora were avid readers and they had brought all their books from the old house, but where they had been previously stored Jacksie had no idea. They were stacked adult-shoulder high all over the house—on landings, on shelves, on window ledges, in hallways, bathrooms, the dining room, sitting room, and bedrooms. Any wardrobe, linen closet, or broom closet had dozens and dozens of books resident—and Jacksie was free to read any and every one of them.

Little Lea was a busy and noisy household because, along with Jacksie and his parents, there was Tim the dog, Tommy the white mouse, Peter the canary, many servants, and deaf Grandfather Lewis. Grandfather shuffled along, shouted when he spoke, loudly sang psalms and Welsh songs, and lived somewhere in the cavernous rooms upstairs. Thus, Jacksie's first priority was to find a suitable space in one of the attics where he could read and write in peace and quiet. Wisely, he claimed the most inaccessible area of all which could only be reached by stepping from one rafter to the next, being ever careful not to slip and put a foot through the ceiling of a lower room. This secret "den" he decorated with colored pictures from Christmas cards, magazines and catalogs together with his own drawings of Animal Land and its characters.

The one blight on Jacksie's otherwise happy existence were the terrible nightmares he suffered of ghosts and creepy-crawlies. With Warren sleeping close by he had felt a degree of comfort. With his brother away, plus the size of the new house with its gurgling pipes, he hated bedtime.

By now his mother was teaching him French and Latin and when Warren arrived home for the long summer holidays, they were able to converse a little in both languages. This brought the brothers even closer and they were so happy to be together again they wanted no interruption from anyone.

Much to their annoyance, though, people insisted they should have other friends. There was a neighbor's son, Arthur Greeves, who was diagnosed when a baby as having a serious heart defect. And although shortly after it was discovered that the diagnosis was a mistake, both Arthur and his mother were so accustomed to the idea that he continued to live like an invalid. This resulted in him being both lonely and bored. He'd often tried to befriend Jacksie and during Warren's vacation his efforts increased. But every day saw the brothers cycling out alone to picnic in the vivid green countryside. They talked of everything and anything, often planning new escapades for either themselves or the fictional characters they would draw or write about in the evenings, up in their secret study.

To Warren, drawing and writing were merely two of many pleasant pastimes. For Jacksie, they meant much more. Although he loved to cycle and swim, he didn't care for any of the other customary boys' pursuits such as football, cricket, or other sports. Much to his disappointment he had already learned that he was completely deficient in manual skills. He longed to make things, but, being large for his age and rather clumsy, things refused to be made. Anything he adamantly forced to be made, fell apart on completion. Even neckties, string and shoelaces blatantly defied him. Either they wouldn't stay knotted, or obstinately remained knotted when he wanted them untied. In view of this, writing and drawing were all he felt capable of.

Those idyllic days with Warren were his idea of heaven. A heaven that had nothing to do with God but related only to the three holidays he spent each year with his adored brother.

Sadly, the heaven never lasted for more than a few weeks. Warren would return to school in England and Jacksie would return to his lonely aerie in the topmost attic of Little Lea. There, until the end of next term, he would while away his time reading more of the thousand books scattered around the house.

One day, on opening yet another of those books, he experienced that same peculiar sensation as when he saw Warren's "toy" garden and again when he discovered autumn. But this time it was words from a Longfellow poem. As he read:

> I heard a voice that cried,
> Balder the beautiful
> Is dead, is dead.
> And through the misty air
> Passed like the mournful cry
> Of sunward sailing cranes. . . .

his heart pounded wildly and the blood raced through his veins. Jacksie didn't know what it meant, yet in his mind was conjured up a whole new world of—of what, he didn't know. He only knew that he was suddenly filled with a yearning for *something* and that if and whenever he encountered it, he would recognize it instantly. This rapture stayed with him for days but eventually it faded to the back of his mind and was forgotten.

2

The Magic Ends

The daily routine continued with lessons from his mother and Miss Harper; letters from Warren and the counting of days until they would be together again.

At the age of nine he didn't pay much attention when the break in his well-organized life first occurred. Grandfather Lewis died suddenly, but as he was a very old man, Jacksie found it easy to accept. He was more disturbed by his uncle's death soon afterward, especially when he saw how deeply affected Albert was at losing both his father and brother in a matter of weeks. It was only when all of that was followed by Flora falling ill with a stomach complaint and having a succession of doctors coming to the house almost daily, that he really began to take notice. Eventually it was decided Flora needed an operation, but instead of going to hospital, a makeshift operating room was made in one of the spare bedrooms. For days Jacksie's nostrils were filled with the smell of ether and disinfectant and he became terrified of the whole idea of operations, illness and pain. Even more distressing was his being kept apart from his mother.

When at last he was taken to see her, she lay pale and still but smiled reassuringly at him. Gradually she gained strength and Jacksie was relieved that she would soon be fully recovered.

It was on a night when he was running a high temperature from a raging toothache that he learned his assumption was wrong. Tossing and turning, he wept with pain and frustration that his mother hadn't come to comfort him. Then he realized the house was full of people again, tramping up and down the stairs, conversing in hushed whispers. How he longed for Lizzie Endicott, his nurse, who had given him so much love and attention while he was little. He also wished that Warren were at home with him.

Later, when the bedroom door was opened, Jacksie sat up half expecting to see his mother but it was his father who came into the room. For a moment Jacksie wondered why he had come to comfort him instead of his mother; then he realized that his father wasn't offering consolation, he was seeking it. Weeping pitifully and ignoring the hour, the child's age, pain and bewilderment, Albert pored out the awful truth. Flora was dying.

Shock numbed the toothache and Jacksie found himself thinking about God, the magician in the sky. Hadn't he been told that God could do all things, if only he was asked? This might be just the time to pray and ask him to make her well again.

From then on, he saw very little of his mother but still he continued to pray. As time went on, he accepted that neither she nor her love were any longer available to him. It was his father who constantly stayed by her sick-bed, and when Warren came home on holiday they were ordered to tiptoe past her room. Only occasionally were they allowed in to see their mother for a short while.

Within weeks of Warren returning to England, Jacksie woke one morning to be told that his mother had died during the night and he was taken to see her.

In cold death she looked nothing like the mother who had held him on her lap, kissed, cuddled and played with him. As for God, well either he hadn't heard Jacksie's prayers or the magic didn't work every time. Perhaps it never worked, he thought cynically. Warren returned home for the funeral. Jacksie, protesting to the last minute, and being forced into his black mourning suit, wanted nothing to do with death, funerals, hearses or wreaths.

Albert neither offered nor even considered that his nine- and twelve-year-old sons needed sympathy over losing their mother. Grief-stricken, he went about crying and bemoaning his own loss. He presented such a pathetic sight, he quite embarrassed his sons, who even became a little afraid of him and avoided him whenever they could. To atone for what they felt was the loss of both their parents, the brothers drew even closer together for warmth and support.

By the time Warren was ready to return to school, Albert, who didn't want the sole respon-sibility of a nine-year-old, arranged for Jacksie to accompany him. Jacksie was grateful. He no longer wanted to stay at Little Lea without either his mother or Warren. However, when it came time to leave there was a certain degree of sad-ness, even though, somehow, Little Lea didn't seem like home anymore.

And neither did Clive Staples Lewis feel like Jacksie anymore, and so he announced that, "From now on I shall be known as Jack."

In this, Albert did reveal a little sentiment towards his son. He simply could not bring him-self to call him by such an adult name, so he alone settled for Jacksie. The cab ride to the Bel-fast docks through the September evening traffic was made in silence by the two boys and their sullen father. Only later, as the ferry moved out from the quayside and into the lough, did they sense his utter dejectedness as he stood alone, waving from the shore.

Once on the open sea, excitement took over the nostalgia as Warren, the seasoned traveler, escorted his young brother over the vessel. But with nightfall, as they climbed into their bunks, Warren became desperately seasick. Convinced that this was the proper way to sail, Jack felt obliged to join him, but it was useless. After much contrived retching he gave up and decided he was as bad at sailing as at making things.

They arrived at Fleetwood, the North Lancashire fishing port, at six-thirty the next morning, with Warren recovering as soon as he stepped from the ferry.

The next part of their journey was by rail to London where they would change trains for Hertfordshire. It was early autumn, Jack's favorite season, but he was dismayed. Instead of the reds, golds and browns he had come to expect, the grasses and trees seemed faded, and in the early morning light everything looked grey. The flat, dull landscape viewed from the carriage windows was totally different from the hills and the sea at home and he instantly developed an intense hatred of England.

Just as when Albert Lewis chose an architect

to design Little Lea, he had shown a similar lack of perception in his choice of school. Three years earlier he had pored over several prospectuses before deciding to send Warren to Wynyard, the school which had produced the best exam results. Oh, he knew there had been a scandalous court case a year earlier when the principal was involved in a brutal attack on a schoolboy—but that had obviously been dealt with, and exam results were exam results. What Albert failed to notice was how extremely out-of-date the records were that he had studied.

During his three years there, Warren had never complained to his parents about Wynyard because he imagined that all public schools were run on similar lines. One must, he believed, simply grin and bear it. There was, however, precious little to grin about.

The school uniform was a tight-fitting bowler hat, heavy boots, a starched, high winged-collared shirt, a thick serge jacket and knickerbocker breeches buttoned so tight at the knees that right through the term there was a permanent red blotch where the button fitted.

The principal, the Reverend Capron, whom the boys nicknamed "Oldie," was a huge man with a long beard and full, fleshy lips. He drank copious amounts of beer, always looked dirty and his behavior was quite bizarre—he would suddenly leap into the air and then prance around the classroom. But, worst of all, he was a psychopathic monster who inflicted, as routine, the most horrendous beatings on his pupils.

His son and colleague, the Reverend John Wynyard Capron, nicknamed "Wyn," was totally different from his father. Although his teaching ability was poor, he was full of good intentions—but, under such oppression, they came to nought.

The food provided for the pupils, Wyn, Oldie's wife and three daughters was barely edible; Oldie sat at a separate table eating food of his own choice. His wife was a timid mouse of a woman. His daughters were never heard to utter more than "Yes, Papa" or "No, Papa," and none of them were ever permitted to wear anything but somber black.

All games at the school had long been abolished. That didn't worry Jack, but it frustrated other more boisterous pupils, Warren being one of them. Lessons were practically non-existent, except for hours of algebra and history during which nothing but strings of meaningless dates were flung at them.

Staff came and went regularly, some staying only a few days. One teacher was threatened that he would be thrown down the stairs for complaining about Oldie's mistreatment of a boy. The building was drab and cold, even in summer. The boys washed in cold water even in winter, and their beds were hard, springless and were situated in cheerless dormitories with bare floors and neither blinds nor curtains at the ceiling-high casement windows. At first in his weekly letters home, Jack begged to be taken away from the "prison camp," but his father ignored him, believing he was merely homesick.

Contrary to other public schools, bullying was unknown amongst Oldie's pupils. There was enough of that from the principal, so, allied against a common foe, the boys treated each other kindly and formed close friendships. Unfortunately, Jack wasn't very good at making friends.

Every Sunday they were taken from the school to church, where they were instructed to pray *consciously* and concentrate on every single word.

Jack's belief in hell was stronger—since his mother's death—than his faith in God or heaven, but now he wondered if she had died because he had not been praying *consciously*.

From then on, each night in the austere dormitory, he knelt on the cold linoleum beside his comfortless bed and prayed with almost inhuman concentration. Each word was mused over before it was said, and, when he'd finished, sure that some words had received more attention than others, he would continue to repeat the prayers until finally, chilled to his bones, he would climb into bed. There, he would reconsider, decide that he still hadn't given full consideration to *every* word, clamber out of bed and begin all over again. This could continue for hours until he felt sick. The next day, weary and exhausted from his nocturnal efforts, he was unable to concentrate on his lessons.

In the end, due to all the energy he put into his prayers, he dreaded bedtime as much for that as for the nightmares he still had of ghosts and monstrous insects.

And yet, if in the dormitory he found extra torment, there were occasions when he found some respite from his awful life. These were when, through the window facing the foot of his bed, he saw fog and snow, thunderstorms and gales that swayed and bent trees under their force. In Ireland, the elements were of a more gentle nature even though there was a more abundant rainfall. On other nights when the moon shone in, casting shadows in its pale light, memories of "Balder is dead" were reawakened. It seemed to him that the very words had painted the vast expanse of black, night sky and cold, white moon. In those moments he wished he could rid himself of the whole burden and misery of Christianity, and be free, instead, to dwell on the magic lantern show of his lively imagination.

Despite his ordeal, at the end of term when they returned to Ireland for the holidays, just like Warren before him, he made no complaint about Wynyard. For the present, the school didn't exist and, if it did, it seemed a million miles away. Why complain anyway? He knew that his father would only half-listen and not understand at all.

Sadly, during those holidays, Albert didn't know what to do with his two lively sons and was thankful his office day lasted from very early morning until evening. This meant of course, that Warren and Jack were left to their own devices and being small boys they often looked for mischief—and usually found it.

Albert was much too refined a man to thrash them as fathers did then, nor did he impose penalties such as forfeiting pocket-money or revoking other privileges. Instead, he chose to lecture them for an hour or perhaps more, and this wasn't always over some serious misdemeanor either. He could scold for an hour over such trivia as leaving a wet towel on the bathroom floor, going into the garden in slippers or failing to hang up a discarded garment.

Ignoring their ages and intellectual capability, he would bewilder them with his extensive vocabulary and quote obscure passages from the great classical scholars and philosophers. The parts he put simply, implied that they would end up penniless, starving and begging for crusts in the street. Or he might even leave them at school all year round and not allow them home for holidays. Or they could even be sent to a penal colony and be put on a chain-gang, for that was surely where they were headed—and all because a wet towel had been left on the bathroom floor.

3

Salvation—of a Sort

D espite Albert's odd ways, the holidays were always enjoyable. Living nearby were some kindly, loving relatives who did everything possible to make up for the boys losing their mother and for their father's eccentricity.

There was Albert's elder brother, jovial Uncle Joe with his jolly brood of three daughters and two sons. There was Flora's brother, Augustus, and his cuddly Canadian wife, Aunt Annie. Uncle Gussie, as he was known to the children, was a brilliant scholar who treated his nephews as equals. In the simplest terms he explained all the obscure mysteries of science and, in easy-to-understand language, regularly discussed current worldly matters.

There was also Flora's mother, Grandmother

Hamilton, a rather dotty, aristocratic old lady who regularly declared that, with the exception of herself, everyone was talking complete nonsense. Her large home was a shambles of dust, clutter and the smell of fifty-odd resident cats. On one day guests would be presented with an excellent meal on chipped, cracked dishes; the next day, burned, inedible food would be served up on Spode or Minton plates.

But of all their relatives, the favorites were cousins Mary and Quartus—formally Sir William Quartus and Lady Mary Warren Ewart. They were an extremely handsome couple with three daughters who were the most beautiful girls Warren and Jack had ever seen. Mary was their mother's cousin, but, as they were more like sisters, after Flora's death she had adopted the role of surrogate mother to her boys. Their stately home, Glenmacken, was an ever-open house where Warren and Jack were free to come and go as they pleased. There was a regular invitation to lunch every Sunday. In addition to providing a second home, the Ewarts took them walking, cycling, motoring, picnicking and to the theater. And from Mary and her daughters, Warren and Jack learned all the manners and graces demanded by society.

Returning to school after the holidays seemed all the worse after their good treatment in Ireland. Once more they would endure the night sail with Warren's ritual seasickness, then the train to Euston and the change for Hertfordshire, each mile taking them closer to Oldie and his "prison-camp."

As much as Jack loathed the place and the man, he had somehow escaped any excessive thrashings, but he could never understand why. Perhaps it was due to Jack's affliction; not that Oldie was merciful, but because he wouldn't want to be held responsible for its aggravation.

For years Jack had been troubled with adenoids—an abnormal growth of glands at the back of the nose which caused a cough, audible breathing and a rather wistful facial expression. Just before his eleventh birthday he was fortunate in having to return home to have them surgically removed. *Fortunate* because it provided a temporary escape from Wynyard even if, recalling his mother's operation, he faced the ordeal with fear. He had another reason to be afraid, too.

The two boys had always shared the same bedroom until Warren went to Wynyard, and Jack, left to sleep alone, was terrified. Now, at school, he had grown used to a dormitory sleeping a dozen or so boys, and the idea of sleeping alone again at Little Lea with its noisy pipes and vast, empty upstairs rooms filled him with horror. His worries were needless though. The operation was a complete success causing little

discomfort and he was soon on his way to recovery. Even better, Albert, probably recalling
Flora's operation, was so concerned for his son
that he gave Jack more attention than he could
ever remember. In case Jack needed him in the
night, Albert even had his son sleeping in his
room. It was quite unnecessary, but he never
knew how grateful Jack was for his company.

During the weeks of convalescence, the father and son drew so close they spent hours
walking in the garden or sitting in the study discussing books. Albert seemed a different man,
and disclosed a clownish sense of humor that
had the boy rolling with laughter.

As Jack was now something of an "invalid,"
and they had something in common, Arthur
Greeves, sent yet another invitation over to Little
Lea, but it was politely declined. Jack preferred
to be with his father. Sadly though, Albert
couldn't see how happy his son was in this new
relationship with a father he thought he'd lost.
He even wrote to Warren saying how sorry he
was, "for Jacko must be desperately bored here
alone with me."

At the same time, Warren was writing home
to say that Mrs. Capron had died suddenly and,
subsequently, Oldie's behavior was worse than
ever.

Before Jack was ready to return to Wynyard,
the Christmas holidays came around and War-

ren arrived home. Now he also benefited from the change in Albert, with his taking them to variety shows and musicals at the theater, then on to restaurants for a late supper before going home. Sadly, in his endeavor to be more companionable towards his sons, he overdid it. Whenever they wanted to be alone with India and Animal Land, he sought them out. If their young cousins came to visit, he stayed there all the time, monopolizing the conversation and generally showing off. This was almost as bad as when he had ignored them.

The holidays drew to an end and the brothers had very mixed feelings. Warren was happy because he was leaving Wynyard for another school, yet sad at leaving his brother. Jack was especially miserable at the prospect of returning alone to Oldie's. Still, there was some mitigation. His cousin, Hope Ewart, was accompanying him to London where she would take him to see "Peter Pan" before depositing him back at Wynyard.

Jack was fascinated by the play about the "boy who never grew up" and wished it could be him. From his father's attitude it seemed that adult life was nought but toil and stress, always worrying over where the next meal was coming from and how long it would be before they were destitute and homeless.

After the theater, he headed back for Oldie's with more trepidation than ever—little knowing how short his stay there would be. Warren's departure for Malvern College left only six boarders at Wynyard, and it was hardly worth keeping open. The following summer, just prior to end of term, the Reverend Capron was whisked away to hospital. His wife's unexpected death the previous year had finally pushed him over the brink; he was declared insane and the school was closed.

When the boys arrived home for the holidays, and Albert heard of Oldie's insanity and saw how obviously relieved Jack was to be away from his establishment, he finally understood what conditions had been like there. Perhaps, he thought, a place closer to home would be more suitable, and began making enquiries. This time, rather than studying prospectuses, he relied on personal recommendation and Jack was sent to where his Uncle Joe's son was extremely happy—the lovely old, red-brick Campbell College in Belfast. This was ideal as he could be a boarder yet spend Sundays at Little Lea. It still meant being separated from Warren, but, in the meantime, they determined to spend every moment they had together.

It was Warren's idea to build a makeshift tent in the garden out of an old sheet and, for the poles, he didn't hesitate to chop up the ladder from the garden shed. At the end of the afternoon when they'd tired of the game, they dismantled the tent, forgot to move the pieces of ladder, and went into the house eagerly awaiting their father's return from the office. By now they had almost forgotten how predictably unpredictable his behavior could be—but they were soon to remember. That evening as all three walked in the garden, Albert's words froze in mid-sentence as he saw and recognized the pieces of timber sticking up in the lawn. He exploded with rage, and, despite Warren owning up, both boys were ordered to the study where they came under one of his old-type tirades.

At first they quaked in their shoes. Then, as he ranted on about how the destruction of the ladder could send them all seeking refuge in the workhouse, it occurred to them both in the same enlightening moment just how silly he sounded and appeared, stalking about the study issuing idle threats.

Warren caught Jack's eye and simultaneously, hiding their faces in their hands, they dissolved in hysterical laughter. Thinking his fifteen- and twelve-year-old sons were convulsed in tears, Albert became even more comical as he fussed around trying to pacify them. By the following day, the crime was forgotten and they were all the best of friends. But from then on all fear of him subsided. Warren and Jack realized that the mercurial temper they had always seen as his strength, was, in fact, a weakness and they loved him more for it.

What a change from Oldie's was Campbell College. In fact, the pupils were so happy and exuberant that after a while Jack found it a bit too lively and noisy. "Like living in a railway station" was how the twelve-year-old described it. An odd feature of the school regarding the juniors was that they had nowhere to go. Unless they were in the dormitory, classroom or refectory, they simply wandered about the building, cluttering up corridors, grouping together on staircases and always being moved on to seek some other place to rest or merely talk together. Unlike Wynyard, there was an element of bullying, but even that was good-natured. New boys under threat would be scared, wondering what their fate was but the "bullying" always turned out to be no more than a trick. One "torture" involved being sent down the coal chute and getting filthy dirty. It usually ended in laughter from both sides.

While he was there, thanks to one excellent teacher, Mr. McNeill—known as Octie—Jack came across the first poet he had ever appreciated, Matthew Arnold. He proved indeed to be a "coiner of sweet words" with his Sohrab and Rustem. The sad story of The Shield of Persia, who never knew that The Smiling One was his son until the moment he slayed him in combat, stirred deep underlying feelings of Jack's relationship with his own father. Albert never seemed to *know* his son.

But consciously, it was the graphic details of the poem that made it an almost tangible thing. It recalled memories of a grim dormitory where, from the window, he saw swirling fog and cool wide spaces. It was as desirable and joyous to him as Warren's "toy" garden, Beatrix Potter's autumn, Barrie's Never Neverland, and those haunting words of Longfellow—Balder is dead. Once more a yearning engulfed him. He felt like an explorer aspiring to reach some far-off goal yet not knowing in which direction to go.

But, no matter where it lay, Jack wasn't directed to it from Campbell College. He didn't even complete his first term. In winter, he developed such a raspish cough—maybe a relapse from the adenoidal surgery—that Albert took him home and, once more, tended to his every need and whim. Again Jack slept in his father's room away from the isolation that evoked his ghosts and beetle nightmares.

During the day, while Albert was at the office, Jack was left free to peruse the mountains of still-unknown books spread all over Little Lea, and to write more stories. These didn't always feature Animal Land now but invariably centered on a fantasy world. He spent so much time dwelling on this other dimension that one day, in the garden, he was sure he'd seen a little, white-bearded gnome in a red, pointed hat scurry across his path and disappear into some bushes.

What would have amazed him more was knowing that Albert was secretly disillusioned by Campbell College. Pleased though he was that "Jacko" was happy, he wanted *his* sons to grow into "perfect gentlemen" and was disappointed at a seemingly marked lack of courtesy and restraint in the boy's manner. This was probably due to early adolescence and a growing independence, but was interpreted by Albert as a lack of discipline at the college. It would be better, he decided, if Jack continued his education with Warren at Malvern in England.

It was almost Christmas again with Warren due home for the holidays. At thirteen, Jack was content to be alone with his brother, relating his most recent stories, and curious to hear what was going on in Warren's "India."

But now, at sixteen-and-a-half, Warren was on the brink of manhood, so, while still interested in Jack's fantasies, he was also taking an interest in the world outside Little Lea and the immediate family.

Because of this growing maturity, and much to Jack's annoyance, invitations began arriving for *both* boys to attend parties and dances which courtesy demanded they accept. At these functions he neither knew nor wanted to know most of the people. He didn't dance, certainly didn't want to indulge in party games organized by the hostess for the "younger ones," and knew nothing about social chit-chat. Bored to distraction, he would sit sulkily observing the silly goings-on, and feeling like hitting the hostess.

Full of bitterness, he would think, *Why ask me? I've never done her any harm. I've never asked her to a party or a dance.* Jack could not imagine people actually attending these events for pleasure. Sometimes a guest, seeing him sitting alone, would feel obliged to go over and keep him company. Then, Jack would brighten up and try to introduce some intelligent conversation into the evening. But after a few of those occasions, he noticed people casting sideways glances at each other, and he realized he was being patronized and humored. They found it amusing to hear this "child" conversing on adult topics in what they assumed was high-falutin' language, when to Jack it was everyday vocabulary. From then on he decided to join in the inane banter going on around him. It placated Albert, Warren, the hostess and her guests, but Jack found it humiliating.

In the early hours of the morning when the ordeal was over, he would clamber thankfully and sleepily into the cab beside his father and brother for the ride home, thinking how wonderful life would be if he and Warren didn't have to grow up.

4

Miss Cowie, Sieved and Wagner

J ack was not particularly upset at leaving
Campbell College for Cherbourg Preparatory School because it meant he would be
close to his brother again. They wouldn't be in
the same building because Malvern College
stood at the bottom of the hill from the prep
school. The one unhappy aspect for Jack was
returning to that hated country England.

Sailing to and fro across the Irish Sea six
times a year, they were by now experienced trav-
elers. This time, instead of Fleetwood, they
sailed on the night ferry to Liverpool, the vast
Lancashire port and cosmopolitan city. There,
they took a cab from the Pier Head to Lime Street
Station but as Warren wanted to display his

adult self-assurance to his young brother, they didn't take the early train to Malvern. The morning was spent browsing through magazines and newspapers in the coffee lounge of the elegant railway hotel on Lime Street, opposite the magnificent St. George's Hall. Later they lunched in the gracious dining-room with Warren displaying even more "manliness" by smoking cigarettes. Jack wasn't impressed by his show of sophistication but didn't say so. Why hurt his feelings? They were together and that was all that mattered.

After lunch, they boarded the train for Malvern in Worcestershire. It was January when England is not at her best and yet as they traveled south Jack was pleasantly surprised at the scenery. It seemed totally different from when he was last in the country, even though it was only a few short months earlier. Of course, it was a different part of the country he was seeing. This journey took the train near to the Welsh border where he looked out on high, snowcapped mountains.

Arriving at the school, the brothers said farewell as Warren got out of the cab and went through the college gates leaving Jack to continue up the hill to Cherbourg. Even before Jack entered the lovely white building, he sensed he would like the place as he looked down the hill toward the town and the Malvern Hills. There were only seventeen boarders, the rest of the pupils being day-boys from nearby. He quickly learned that there were the usual cliques, fights and grumbles at everything, including the good food, good housing and good teachers. In effect, Cherbourg was a normal boys' school. And for once—maybe due to the wonderful atmosphere in the place—Jack soon made several friends.

The staff were all individual characters whom Jack warmed to. The headmaster, Arthur Allen, was known affectionately as "Tubbs" and under his guidance, within weeks, Jack's English and Latin improved enormously.

He even put in extra effort for the mathematics teacher, but, although his mother had degrees in both subjects, math and algebra remained unlearnable foreign languages to him.

One teacher, "Sirrah" as he was known, was so jolly and youthful in his attitude toward the boys that Jack started taking an interest in outdoor activities which, other than cycling, walking and swimming, he'd always disliked. Now he began running purely for pleasure. With Sirrah everything could be made enjoyable, even jogging in atrocious weather.

Added to this was another much-sought-after achievement—he finally managed to rid himself of his scant Christian beliefs.

Had he not settled in so well, he would have turned for solace to Miss Cowie, every boys' dream of what a school matron should be and rarely is. She may have appeared middle-aged to the boys but was really little more than a girl. Cheerful yet tender, efficient while being full of sympathy, fun but with common sense, she reminded Jack of his childhood nurse. She also had a similar mind, but, while Lizzie Endicott was obsessed by myths and legends, Miss Cowie was immersed in different religious faiths. And with a youthful lack of discretion she innocently discussed them with her worshipping charges.

She had dabbled in spiritism where people believe they can communicate with the dead, Tarot cards which are supposed to foretell the future, and Buddhism and Hinduism—religions of the East. Not even Rosicrucianism, the belief that matter can be magically changed into different forms, had escaped her.

Perhaps with relief at leaving Oldie's, and perhaps due to improved relations with his father, the intensity of Jack's praying had eased off during the past year. He no longer needed help from God so there was no need to be on such good terms with him. So, while the school matron was simply exploring all possibilities while denying none, Jack happily relieved himself of his Christian faith.

Floundering about in a confusion of half beliefs, he began reading the sort of literature that covered every conceivable faith. While readily rejecting those where human or animal sacrifice was demanded, he questioned the validity of all others—particularly Christianity. Why in books by Christian authors were all other beliefs dismissed as mere illusion, fairy tales and myths? Why were they treated as a huge joke, while Christianity was respected and accepted as the true one with Christ the one true God? He hadn't saved Jack's mother.

Since going to Cherbourg he had read and learned more about man's inhumanity to man, of all the cruelty in the world—and that alone, he decided, posed questions as to whether Christ was all-powerful. This shedding of his religion lifted a great burden from his young shoulders and he seemed rid of all care. As that first year at Cherbourg drew to a close, he heard that both Sirrah and Miss Cowie were leaving and wouldn't be back next term. At this news his lightheartedness was replaced with an emptiness he hadn't known since his mother died.

His only comfort was in meeting up with Warren again to set off for Ireland and the Christmas holidays. On the train journey north, Jack felt quite the seasoned traveler. He was bordering on his fourteenth birthday and catching up quickly with his brother. Arriving at Liverpool they had supper at the Lime Street Hotel, then went next door to see a variety show at the Empire Theater. Jack didn't care for light entertainment, but he did like the atmosphere of stage, footlights and costumes. While all about him were laughing and applauding, he was staging productions in an imaginary world of his own.

After the show, they took the late-night ferry to Belfast where he faced the unwelcome social round of parties and dances, but now he was able to handle the situations somewhat better. Again Arthur Greeves asked the boys over and as usual they made excuses not to go.

Jack didn't enjoy the time at home as much as he'd anticipated—not even his fourteenth birthday in November. Right through the holidays he kept trying to visualize Cherbourg without Sirrah and the matron, and it was with a heavy heart that he returned to Malvern. Once there he was pleasantly surprised. Sirrah's replacement was a wonderful man—if not the most desirable of tutors for such young and impressionable minds.

To Jack and his classmates, "Pogo" was extremely sophisticated and worldly-wise. In reality, his charisma came from his assumed air of worldly wisdom. He was extremely young—fresh from university and longing to prove to his naive pupils, who were only a few years his junior, how very grown up he was.

Pogo knew the words to all the "pop" songs. Pogo knew all the scandals about show-business people. He knew how to dress in tasteless, flashy style with his over-sized jackets, wide, wide colorful ties, too broad shoelaces and brilliantly hued socks.

Jack knew from Warren that some of the Malvern College boys had already adopted this style, but he hadn't been impressed until now. With his senses in a vacuum, he was open to any suggestion that would lead him away from tradition and convention. Consequently, his one aim was to emulate his mentor, Pogo. This wasn't easy for someone with a weekly allowance of one shilling. It was of further hindrance when that someone was a bulky, overgrown fourteen-year-old with a hefty walk who always looked as though his clothes had come from a rag-man's cart. Still, he did his best by plastering his hair down with grease and constantly pressing his trousers.

Reason returned most unexpectedly one day when Jack chanced by a magazine bearing reference to a book called *Siegfried and the Twilight of the Gods*. If those few words caused his spirit to soar, their accompanying illustration swept away the emptiness from his soul. Those half-forgotten words "Balder is dead" came back over the years, repeating themselves over and over again in his mind. From somewhere into his head came a thunderous crescendo of stirring music and a vision of clean, pure, northern space. He didn't understand what was happening, yet instinctively knew they all related to *Siegfried and the Twilight of the Gods*.

The *lightness* he'd felt in his heart was suddenly recognized as cold and darkness. Now light and warmth were flooding back into him as though a harsh winter had melted instantly into spring. Snow and ice were replaced by trickling water, birdsong, blossoming primroses and violets. At last Joy was rediscovered.

5

Joy Recaptured

*F*rom that one inspiring moment, Jack shook off all muddled ideas of various religious faiths to pursue *The Twilight of the Gods.* He learned that Balder was the son of Odin and god of peace, virtue and light who was killed by the cunning of Loki, once a friend of the gods, now their foe.

Odin was the Norse god of war and learning, creator of earth, sky and all mankind. Siegfried was a dragon-slayer and beloved of Brunhild, chief of the Valkyries, Odin's warrior maidens who flew over battlefields choosing those to be slain. In death, the slain heroes were taken over Bifrost, the rainbow bridge leading to Asgard, home of the gods where they would be feasted in Valhalla, one of Asgard's banqueting halls.

These discoveries rendered Balder, Siegfried

and Odin more true and vital to him than Christ had ever been, yet, without question, Jack accepted it all as mere legend. This showed in a growing fascination of the gods' creators—the earthly Norsemen and their lands of pine forests and wolves, where night and day lasted for half of the year. He yearned to see the Aurora Borealis and longed even more to learn the ancient Norse language.

From then on, he seemed destined to have one revelation after another presented to him. The first came during his holidays in Ireland.

For Christmas that year Albert had bought his sons a gramophone, although Jack possessed little knowledge of music and showed even less interest in it. While Warren scrutinized every record catalog he could find, Jack displayed no more than a passing interest in any his brother left lying about. That is until the day his gaze fell upon a certain name, Wagner. He'd never heard of the composer and yet something about the very word *Wagner* echoed that elusive "Northerness" by which he was so tormented.

Sitting down to read the catalog more thoroughly he gasped to see that particular reference was the synopsis for a grand opera—"The Ring of the Nibelung." Jack's heart leaped, for there staring out from the page, were those magic words, Siegfried and Brunhild.

The records were bought and he listened in

rapture to the dramatic music he had first heard in his mind. They were sounds that raised his spirit to great heights, evoking scenes of grandeur, wilderness and loneliness in the vast northern spaces.

Later in the holidays, he visited his newly married cousin, Hope Ewart, and there, laying on a coffee table in her home, was a copy of *Siegfried and the Twilight of the Gods*, the very book he'd seen listed in the magazine at Cherbourg. Page after page reflected precisely all he'd imagined and possession of the book became imperative.

Checking the inside cover, he saw its price was prohibitive to someone whose life savings stood at about one dollar. His unspoken longing must have conveyed itself to Warren though. He took the trouble to trace a cheaper edition costing about $1.50 and gave Jack half the money toward what he considered was simply "an attractive picture book."

Elation surged through Jack as he gazed at the illustrations while listening to his recordings of Wagnerian might. Now he didn't want only to absorb and possess this wonder; there was a desire to give out something that was building up inside him. He could never compose the music to express his emotions—but he could write.

From then on every spare moment was spent

in writing, writing, writing. Short stories, books and poems poured out of him; some good, some not, but it didn't matter. They brought him Joy.

In June 1913, when he was fifteen, it was time to take his entrance scholarship for Malvern College and he was ill in the school sanatarium with a high temperature. Both Jack and the teaching staff were so disappointed that his doctor made a hasty decision. If the papers were taken over to Cherbourg he could take the exam from his sickbed.

Under those circumstances it was no slight achievement when he gained the scholarship with exceptionally high grades. However, before starting at "the Coll," as Malvern College was known, the long and leisurely summer holidays in Ireland with Warren lay ahead.

During the two years he was at Cherbourg, the "preps" were often taken to the college for sports days or to cheer on a college team against a visiting school. Jack was always so proud of his athletic brother on those occasions, and longed for the time when they would be together for the final years of their education. But it wasn't to be.

With the exception of the first few months at Oldie's, those three-and-a-half years difference in their ages always determined that they be kept apart. As Jack was about to enter the college at the bottom of the hill, Warren, in only his third year, was leaving.

His intentions had always been to go straight from Malvern to the military academy at Sandhurst for training as an Army officer. But for some time, Albert had been concerned about both his progress at school and his general attitude, especially towards discipline at home. The age gap between the brothers was quite distinct now, with Jack still obviously a boy and Warren a young man. At eighteen-and-a-half Warren had become rude and surly. His school reports were abysmal and, in despair, Albert took him away from Malvern. For his final year he would take an intensive study course with William Kirkpatrick, Albert's own former tutor from Lurgan College. Known as the "Great Knock," he was now retired and living in England at Surrey.

After weeks of cycling and picnicking in the glorious Irish countryside, hours of reading, writing and listening to Wagner, it was time to return to England. Warren was heading for the home of the Great Knock and Jack to Malvern College where, he was assured, nothing but happiness awaited him. But Malvern was totally different from what Jack had expected. If Campbell was boisterous and noisy, the Coll was doubly so. And of course, as at many public schools, there were Bloods and Fags.

Bloods were senior pupils of up to nineteen

years of age. They were either prefects, sports idols or simply admired by the other students— not necessarily for their social or charitable qualities. In practice they were nothing other than school bullies and were, almost without exception, sadists. Fags on the other hand were the most junior newcomers and were acknowledged by pupils and staff as Bloods' slaves.

Concentration on games and physical prowess, which Jack loathed, were *de rigueur*. Favorite conversational topics were cricket and rugby and it was obligatory to rave over them whether as a participant or spectator.

Always seeing himself as a great, hulking, beefy lout, Jack understood why others assumed he would be bored by such masculine pursuits. He did contrive a show of enthusiasm but it must have been badly portrayed and he was soon a labeled target for the Bloods. Once he was flogged for failing to present himself for games over a period of two weeks after a Blood named Fribble deliberately and repeatedly gave him the wrong team, days and times to appear.

As a scholarship student, Jack was automatically placed in a class higher than his age group where he found trouble enough keeping up with the rest. Add to this the fact that he was constantly being fagged to clean shoes, clean desks, make tea, clean sports equipment, and other demeaning tasks. His work deteriorated because he was denied so much study time. It wasn't unknown for an unpopular boy to be "fagged" as a means of ensuring he was late for class, or missed it altogether. Obviously this meant getting into trouble with the tutor and sometimes resulted in a flogging from the Headmaster.

Sanctuary was granted only in the "Gurney," their name for the Coll library. Once in there, no one could be fagged. But gaining entrance was a feat of cunning coupled with luck. Like predators, Bloods lay in wait for prey and with one hand on the Gurney doorknob a boy could still be claimed for hours and hours of fagging.

Peace was non-existent and Jack's life was a misery. Again his weekly letters home begged his father to take him away from the wretched place and, as at Wynyard, they were ignored.

Warren had loved his time at the Coll but as he went there direct from Wynyard, after Oldie's regime, anything would have been an improvement. A gregarious and robust character, he had involved himself in all manner of physical activity and as a junior had stoically accepted the inevitable fagging. By comparison, after Oldie's, Jack had experienced the happy-go-lucky existence at Campbell followed by an almost pampered period at Cherbourg before being plunged into the Coll.

On hearing from Albert that Jack detested Malvern, Warren was astonished. Just before

Christmas when he returned for an old boys' re-union and learned from the Bloods how unpopular his bookish, introverted brother was, he was angry and felt let down. At Warren's fury, Jack feared his most precious, personal relationship was threatened. There had never been an unhappier time in his life. Exhausted from fagging and worried over his brother's attitude towards him, he would collapse into bed at night so weary and distressed that he wished he would never wake up.

Nevertheless, the rigors of Malvern did have some compensations. One was when he, and a few boys of similar mind, could escape for a couple of hours to roam the Malvern Hills, basking in their surroundings. Another was having for his Upper Fifth form master, Harry Wakelyn Smith, teacher of Classics and English.

"Smewgy," as he was known, was a tall, unattractive man with grey hair, grey face and bulbous eyes, but his voice was like sweet music. In such a hostile environment he stood out like a guiding beacon. Always courteous, calling his students "gentlemen," it was impossible for even the most reluctant to show him anything but respect.

In Jack Lewis, Smewgy saw promise of a great classical scholar and encouraged him in his writing. And with Smewgy, for a while, Jack was able to forget the horrors awaiting him on the other side of the classroom door. Like a lost desert traveler, he clung to this tiny oasis of sanity while his mentor unveiled worlds as alien to him as Norse gods had once been.

There was Zeus, the great Greek god equivalent of Odin; tragic Thetis, loved by both Zeus and his brother, Poseidon, but betrayed by them for power and given in marriage to Peleus. There were Priam and Paris, Achilles, Helen, Apollo, Aphrodite, Heracles, Hera—the names spilled out and Jack's thirst for more knowledge increased.

Then just as he declared that longing insatiable, he encountered yet another world swirling about in the mists of mythology. This recalled cozy nights in the nursery with Warren nestled up close to Lizzie Endicott, being enthralled by her tales of Celtic deities and legends.

He learned that, rather than gods the Celts worshipped goddesses—nearly all of whom were dedicated to motherhood through Anu, "mother of the gods." Also there was Cailleach Bheara who made the mountains, Caleena and Bevill who chased away the "demons of sickness," and Brigit the "herald of spring and guardian of the hearth."

More and more Jack retreated from the "real" world into the wild lands of the Norse gods, the lily strewn Elysian Fields of the Greeks, his own

Celtic heritage or, quite simply, into the lands of his own making.

Animal Land and India still existed, but now they were Jack's own dominions. Warren had outgrown Boxon even though it had, by then, acquired adult-fantasy stature. It's parliament, Damerfesk, was ruled over by the littlemaster or prime minister who, in that year, 1913, happened to be a frog.

All of this became so real and wholesome in preference to the outside world that there were times when Jack was living as two people. There could be the odd good day at Malvern, yet he couldn't appreciate it if some other world was having serious problems. Alternatively, one of the darkest days at the Coll could be tolerated if a mythological character from ancient legend or Boxon had overcome some obstacle.

6

Back to Earth

When the Christmas holidays came around, pleased as Jack was at returning to Ireland away from this hated college, he was worried about the reception he would get from Warren.

Warren was anxious over the reception he would get from his father, but Albert was overjoyed when he read his end-of-term report. Mr Kirkpatrick wrote that so much progress had been made in those few months, he suspected Warren had learned absolutely nothing at Malvern. This caused Albert to reflect on the letters he received every week from Jack pleading to be taken away from the Coll.

Sadly, conditions at home between father and sons had begun to deteriorate again. Although Albert was taking them to the theater and generally entertaining them with his great sense of humor, in his endeavor to be a good father, he overdid everything. He persisted in inflicting his company on the boys when it was least wanted, and seemed unable to communicate with them when it was most needed. Although Jack received none, mail for his brother arrived almost daily from old Malvern friends and Kirkpatrick, and Albert demanded to read every letter. As a silent protest against this intrusion the boys conspired to hide the letters before their father found out that the postman had arrived.

Another irritating facet of Albert's nature was that he constantly misconstrued facts. Something related to him could, by the next day, or hour, have names, dates and incidents so changed as to bear no resemblance to the original story. Yet he would insist they were precise in every detail.

To Jack this was almost as wearing as fagging. To Warren it was infuriating. Guiltily, they avoided their father just as when they were small boys and sighed with relief when he left for the office.

During that holiday the three-and-a-half-year age gap between the brothers began to make itself evident. Once they were together again the anger of one and the anxiety of the other was forgotten, but despite that they had little in common.

In the past, Jack had been contented at Little Lea while his brother was at school. But writing and drawing alone in the attic room wasn't the same when Warren was absent by choice. The distance in their relationship left him feeling utterly lost, yet, ironically, this worked in his favor which he was soon to discover.

When yet another invitation came from their neighbor's son, Arthur Greeves, although at nineteen he was Warren's age, it was Jack who accepted it. He reasoned that Arthur, being an invalid with for older brothers and sisters, might, at times, feel lonely and rejected.

Half-heartedly but with a degree of sympathy he went over to the Greeves house and was shown into Arthur's room where, as usual, he was convalescing from some illness. But even before Jack looked at the sickly young man propped up by a mountain of pillows, his eyes lighted on a book resting on the bedside table— *Myths of the Norsemen*.

Simultaneously both said, "Do *you* like that?" With those words their friendship was established and Jack spent the rest of his holiday with Arthur. For hours they discussed their favorite Norse gods and legends. But these weren't Arthur's sole interest. He painted, played the piano, composed music and was at that time working on an opera about "Loki." He also encouraged Jack to widen his reading interests, taking in the Brontes, Jane Austen, Sir Walter Scott and Hans Andersen.

Jack had unwittingly adopted a rather snobbish attitude toward nature—admiring the distant, the grand, the majestic and the unattainable. Only the highest mountain, the pale moon, the sky and cloud formations or the power of the ocean moved him. And though Arthur shared this wonder with him, he could find fulfillment in, what he called, the hominess around him. The grass and flowers at his feet, fruit bushes, trees and the birds that visited or nested in them. There was even beauty in a plot of rich, brown soil crowned by green cabbages. Such observations brought Jack back to solid earth reminding him of the Joy he'd known from Warren's toy garden and Beatrix Potter's autumn.

Arthur was naturally delighted that, at last, he'd made contact with one of the Lewis boys, and Jack was more than pleased at this new friendship. It would provide mental escape from the Coll because they could write to each other about their mutual interests. He would have been even happier had he known the letters wouldn't be written from Malvern.

Throughout the holiday Albert pondered over both the Great Knock's comments concerning Warren, and Jack's complaints of the school. He had ignored the boy's awful reports of Oldie's establishment only to discover later that they were correct. What if he was making the same mistake again? When asked for his opinion, Warren still stinging from the humiliation of his brother's unpopularity at Malvern, advised his father to let him leave.

The week the boys were due back in England, Albert approached Jack with a proposition he felt sure he would only partly approve of. "How would you like to leave Malvern and go for special tuition to Mr. Kirkpatrick as Warren has done?" he asked.

Jack was speechless for a moment and, thinking he'd been right in his doubts, his father added, "That is if you would be happy there, living quietly with an elderly couple out in the country, away from other boys your age?"

At this, Jack quickly recovered from the shock. Happy! Would he be happy in the quiet countryside away from boys of his own age! It was like asking somebody if they would be happy without toothaches or frostbite. It would be like going over the rainbow bridge to Valhalla or to the Elysian Fields or being pampered by Anu, mother of the gods.

He was to complete his year at Malvern and then, after the summer recess, would travel to the home of his father's former tutor at Surrey in England. Warren would be at Sandhurst before then so once again they would be separated. However, Jack was accustomed to that by now and returned to Malvern counting the days to the Easter holidays, the summer term and then blessed July.

Although the school authorities must have known he was leaving, he kept the knowledge from the enemy—the Bloods. Having that secret made his impending departure all the more delectable.

In May of that year, 1914, ugly rumors of a threatened outbreak of war between Germany and Britain began circulating. Warren was almost twenty and had been at Sandhurst since Easter. If war was declared he would be among the first to be involved, a fact which gave his brother much cause for concern although he tried to put it at the back of his mind.

At last, the Malvern nightmare came to an end and Jack was packing his belongings for the last time to go home to Ireland. His one regret was leaving Smewgy. But if the Great Knock was all he was reputed to be, his year ahead of concentrated education would compensate for that loss. Once more he was crossing the Irish Sea, heading for Belfast, Arthur Greeves, Little Lea and his father. Warren was on leave at the time, so, just as throughout their childhood, they traveled together. Nevertheless, this wasn't the totally happy occasion it should have been. Rumors abounded and war seemed imminent; hence the leave from Sandhurst in preparation for what inevitably lay ahead. It was deeply disturbing, but, for the time being, they were together and Jack had escaped the Coll.

As soon as he arrived home, Jack's father began inundating him with supposedly helpful advice and anecdotes concerning Kirkpatrick's school—much of which Jack found disturbing. There were glowing reports of how soft-hearted and physically affectionate he could be. Apparently when Albert was feeling down one day, the old man had actually placed his arm about him and brushed his face with his whiskers. The threat of any repetition filled Jack with revulsion. There were hints of other unpleasant experiences he could expect to undergo such as "interesting adult conversation" meaning, of course, politics, religion and ailments.

The more Albert raved over his former teacher, the more doubtful Jack became and groaned inwardly. Warren had loved Malvern while he had hated it. Albert idolized the Great Knock yet he thought his father's friends pompous and boring. Would his time at Surrey turn out to be as disappointing as the Coll, he wondered? Even so, it seemed preferable to endless fagging by the sadistic Bloods.

7

The Great Knock

O n August 4, Great Britain declared war
on Germany. Warren was ordered to report immediately to the military camp at
Aldershot in England, and the brief happy in-
terlude in Ireland came to an abrupt end. Albert
and Jack went to Belfast to see him off, both wondering and worrying over what the future held,
with neither daring to voice their fears.

One Friday evening a few weeks later, Jack,
too, was on his way, if not, like his brother, to
face danger, at least into the unknown.

On reaching Liverpool he didn't bother to
have breakfast at the Lime Street Hotel as he
would have with Warren. Instead, he took the
first train to Waterloo Station in London and
from there a train going south towards the Kirk-
patricks' home, Gastons at Great Bookham in

Surrey. The whole rustic coziness of the county appealed to him instantly. Gentle hills, ponds, green hedges, wicket gates and fences, red-tile-roofed farmhouses and thatched white cottages half hidden in leafy lanes. He drank in scene after varying scene, acknowledging it was due to Arthur's influence that he appreciated such hominess.

At the station he was met by the revered Kirkpatrick and here was another surprise. The Great Knock was not the benign little grandfather figure he had imagined. Aged sixty-six and over six feet tall, he was lean and muscular with an iron handclasp. A bristly beard and side whiskers emphasized the total baldness of his shiny head. He wore the shabbiest of suits, his voice was rather gruff and his manner a little brusque which, Jack feared, probably hid a lot of pent up emotion. Would the Great Knock embrace him and caress his face with his whiskers? Jack thought with a shudder.

For the first time in his life, despite his bulk, he felt quite small and neat seated beside the huge, unkempt man in the taxi heading for Gastons. He also felt distinctly uncomfortable and inadequate in such a presence. After some minutes had passed, adopting the same routine of "small talk" learned at those awful dances and parties, he said, "I'm surprised at the scenery. Surrey is much wilder than I'd imagined!"

"Stop!" roared Kirkpatrick, nearly startling Jack out of his wits. "What do you mean by wilder and why should you not expect it?" Jack stammered an inane reply which was followed by another "Stop! On what have you based your assumptions? By reading? Studying maps, perhaps? Talking to the natives?"

Jack mumbled another equally provocative answer by saying he hadn't done any of those, he'd simply formed opinions. "Never form opinions. Use logic," ordered Kirkpatrick and again began questioning him. It was then Jack realized the Great Knock wasn't being difficult, he was genuinely interested; he really wanted to know. The cram course had already begun.

Jack had never met a man more given to logic. Every remark, every statement was followed by "Stop!" or *"Excuse me!"* It was then dissected and analyzed to point out its futility. More favorably was "I hear you," which meant, "Continue. So far you are doing all right."

Jack recognized that some people might take exception to this attitude, but he reveled in it. As for the adult talk on politics, religion and ailments, he suspected Kirkpatrick would avoid it as eagerly as himself.

But where was the man his father had described? The explanation came to him in a flash. As usual, Albert had got it all wrong. He hardly knew the man he'd spent so much time with and admired above all others. As for the embrace and whisker rubbing? That was probably from his own father when he was a small child—still in his crib maybe.

That evening he got to know and like Kirkpatrick's wife Louise, who was, from necessity, an extremely patient and tolerant woman. He also discovered his tutor considered it foolish to speak unless one had something worth saying, and that he had a passion for gardening.

Sunday was spent getting to know the house, the gardens and the surrounding lanes. He noticed Kirkpatrick was gardening in a much smarter suit than he'd worn the previous day, yet he made no mention of going to church. Later Jack learned that he was an atheist despite a strict Presbyterian upbringing. Nevertheless, he always wore the good suit on Sundays.

On Sunday evening, Jack was given his schedule and curriculum. Breakfast was at eight o'clock. Work in his own private, little study upstairs was from nine until one, with a short coffee break at eleven. Lunch was from one to two, and then the afternoon was free to do exactly as he pleased. After tea at four-fifteen, it was back to work at five until dinner at seven. The rest of the evening was free with bed at eleven. Sundays were completely free days.

This orderly arrangement spelled perfection to Jack but the next announcement seemed more of a threat when Kirk declared, "Tomorrow morning we begin to read Homer."

Oh, golly, he thought, and recalling the few lines he knew of Pod's translation of the *Iliad* he wondered, has this *"started a myriad sufferings," "Of woes unnumbered"*?

The next morning at nine sharp, student and tutor opened their identical copies at *Iliad* Book I, from which Kirk read aloud one hundred lines with barely a pause for explanation. When he'd finished, he told Jack to read the passage again and translate as much as he could. Then, handing him a lexicon—Greek dictionary—he left the room. For a while Jack gaped wide-eyed at the book resting in his lap. He was convinced it would take as long to translate the *Iliad* as it took the siege of Troy itself—ten years. However, gritting his teeth, he began, and by eleven o'clock he was surprised at how much he'd mastered. His teacher wasn't surprised—it was no more than he had expected from such a potentially brilliant scholar.

Kirk followed the pattern every morning and each day Jack managed more until eventually he was translating every one of the hundred lines. Spurred on by this, almost as a challenge, he began to read and translate more work than Kirk had assigned. His mentor made no comment, for Jack wasn't to know this was his particular teaching method.

After some weeks had passed, Jack announced one day that he was no longer translating but was actually thinking in Greek. "*Naus*" didn't *mean* "a ship." It *was* a ship.

Kirk gave one of his rare smiles and told him, "That is the only way to learn a language." In a letter to Albert, he said that Jack was the best Greek translator he had ever met, adding "He uses words and phrases I would never think of."

As the months went by, Jack grew increasingly happy with his work, his tutor and with his environment. Even with the organized routine and the intellectual stimulation, there was always a relaxed atmosphere at Gastons. On the other hand, holidays in Ireland were a mixture of pleasure and stress.

Considering the time he had spent in England, the years had actually brought him closer to family and friends and they all had a better understanding of each other. They gathered at each other's houses for hours of pleasant, often humorous conversation. By now his dislike of parties and dances was respected and people stopped issuing unwanted invitations. Sadly, relations with his father were getting worse. As Jack spent every day with Arthur Greeves, Albert demanded that every evening and weekend be spent with him. He insisted on reading every letter his son received from Warren or Kirkpatrick, but, worst of all, with Jack's increased powers of logic and clear thinking, Albert's conflicting and confusing conversations were more exasperating than ever.

On Warren's few leaves from France he would collect Jack from Bookham and they would sail over to Ireland to share the precious time together. How proud Jack was of his officer brother, yet he had no inclination to join him in the service.

In Warren's letters he often named those who had been lost in battle; old Wynyard boys; Cherbourg boys; Malvern boys; both Fags and Bloods. But over the terrible events in war-torn France, Jack assumed Kirk's logic. He refused to think about, read or listen to war stories. It was futile to become involved in something he had no power to change.

Warren's regiment wasn't on the front line, so his family had no great cause to worry, yet, subconsciously, Jack was concerned. His insect nightmares were replaced by more macabre ones. In his dreams he heard his brother walking about in the garden under his bedroom window, always he was trying to call to him but no sound came, nor was Jack able to answer him.

In 1916, when he was seventeen, and events in France were at their most grim, compulsory military service was introduced in England. Being Irish, Jack was exempt, but being logical he had accepted for some time that a day might come when he would have to go to war.

He'd been with Kirkpatrick for two years, and after conquering thirteen books of the *Iliad* and nine of the *Odyssey*, the idyllic Gastons period was coming to an end.

In spite of his meager mathematical ability, he hoped to go on from Bookham to university, probably to become tutor. He also wanted to be a writer, but of what he wasn't sure, so, concerned with his immediate future, he made a solemn pact with England. "You shall have me on a certain date, not before. I will die in your wars if need be, but till then I shall live my own life. You may have my body but not my mind. I will take part in battles but not read about them."

Passing through London on his way to and from Ireland he was noticing ever-increasing numbers of uniformed men on the trains and at stations, and he realized that "certain date" with destiny was rapidly drawing nearer.

One evening he confided to his father that, although he wasn't afraid and was prepared to die for England, he was so concerned at the prospect that he could barely concentrate on his studies. The implication that he might lose his son evaded Albert completely. He embarked upon a lecture on the virtue of hard work, the importance of education, the cost of his education to date and that, in old age, he would be unable to provide for him so he must continue his studies to secure a prosperous future.

Jack thought wryly that in view of the casualty figures coming out of France, he may not have a future but it was pointless to reiterate.

Regarding Jack's future, Albert wrote to Kirk that he hoped Jack would either join the regular army, take up law, go to university and obtain a fellowship or become a schoolteacher. Kirk's reply was, "He will be either a writer or a tutor, don't try to make him anything else."

It was his eighteenth year, and during that holiday his father reminded him it was time he was confirmed in the church. This presented Jack with a dilemma he'd never even considered. To admit he was a non-believer would not only incur Albert's wrath, it would also offend friends and relatives, as being confirmed was "the thing to do" in their social circle. But, he reasoned, solemnly *acting out a ritual*—committing himself to, what was after all, just another mythology could do no harm and would avoid unpleasant confrontations. On this decision he was confirmed into the Church and then furthered the blasphemy by taking communion.

Later, he was amazed to find himself questioning his theory. Did he really shy away from admitting his atheism to avoid offending others or did it go deeper? Why was there an element of guilt lurking in the back of his mind? Without really being aware of it, for some time Norse gods and Wagner had been losing their enchantment. It was as though by studying both subjects in great depth and gaining immense knowledge of them he had obliterated all sense of spontaneous Joy.

In their place, perhaps because of his nightmares about Warren, there was an unhealthy fascination for the morbid and macabre aspects of Greek mythology—Hades and Tartarus, Acheron, Lethe and Styx, Pluto and Charron had all usurped cumulus, cirrus and the clear, white spaciousness of the Norse lands. There was a growing interest in the occult and wizardry to a point where, had he known of a local witch, he would have been tempted to contact her.

By now he had taken Kirk's logic to its extreme. A table was a table. A cup was a cup. Life was life. Death ended all. Materialism was fact, all else was myth. Yet, if all faiths were mere myths, why pursue the occult? Why when he was a materialist, he thought angrily, did his subconscious persist in being so foolishly illogical?

8

From Oxford to Hell

Throughout his schooldays, Oxford had been Jack's ultimate goal and on December 4, 1916, just one week after his eighteenth birthday, he was due to sit for the scholarship. If he passed he could then join the University Officer Training Corps (U.O.T.C.) and obtain a commission before enlisting in the army.

His arrival in the historic city, however, was disappointing. It was a bitterly cold day, but thinking he would find lodgings near the station, he decided to go on foot rather than take a hansom cab (two-wheeled horse-drawn carriage). On and on he walked through unlovely, grey streets wondering where the reputedly beautiful buildings were? Were they another myth?

After a while, he knew something was wrong

as the houses and shops began to thin out and ahead of him lay open country. Utterly perplexed, he placed his luggage on the ground and turned to look back along the street: only then did he realize he had been walking in the wrong direction. There, on the distant skyline, were Oxford's "dreaming spires and towers" surrounding the dome of Radcliffe Library, Gibbs' architectural masterpiece.

Just then a cab was passing, and hailing it he wearily instructed the driver to "Take me to where I can find a comfortable bed for the night." Within a few minutes he was deposited at the door of some good, homey lodgings close to the University.

It snowed throughout the night and by morning the high pinnacles and rooftops of the University buildings had taken on the appearance of an ornate wedding cake. When Jack emerged from his lodgings to make his way to the Hall of Oriel for his scholarship, right there and then he fell in love with Oxford.

It was still snowing when he arrived at the hall and, as there was no fuel for heating due to wartime shortages, the entrants were permitted to take their exams in overcoats, scarves and gloves. Numb with cold, Jack somehow struggled through the set essay on Samuel Johnson. Only afterward, when he heard others discussing what they had included, was he convinced that he had failed miserably.

The following day he left for Ireland, dreading having to tell his father his suspicions. Yet surprisingly, Albert sympathized with him and even encouraged him to put it out of his mind until after Christmas. However, in the Christmas Eve post, along with the last of the greeting cards, came word that he had passed the scholarship and been accepted for possible entry to University College. All that remained now was the entrance exam proper, Responsions, which included maths and algebra.

In this, he really did fail miserably, but, as all his other results were good, he was advised to do some intensive study and try again. Once more he headed for Gastons and Kirkpatrick for a one-term cram course in the hated subjects.

Always while at Bookham, one afternoon each week—summer or winter—he would take the train into Leatherhead. There he would get his hair cut, go for a dip in the swimming baths and then browse around the bookshops. On a particularly miserable February evening while waiting for the train "home" to Gastons he noticed, reduced in price on the railway bookstall, a begrimed edition of George MacDonald's *Phantasies*. MacDonald was an unknown poet to him, but relishing the idea of a bargain and a cozy evening of reading until bedtime, he bought the book.

That night, as he began reading the small, grubby volume a long lost emotion started sweeping over him. Although there were evils and wrongdoers in the story, the gentle fairy romance recalled the innocence of Shakespeare's *Midsummer Night's Dream*, Barrie's *Peter Pan* and Beatrix Potter's *Squirrel Nutkin*. Something good, sweet, wholesome and full of simple *hominess* lay within those pages, and Jack suddenly realized how far he had slipped along the downward path of despair. Even his tea-time reading, which he always reserved purely for pleasure, had seen him forsake Jane Austen, Walter Scott and Hans Andersen for the more depressing Ibsen.

The comfort seeping into him from those pages was like convalescing after a serious illness and he determined never to tread those dark ways again. He was unable to find his way back to Wagner or Norse with its clean, pure space, yet he knew in his heart there was goodness and light to be found—somewhere.

After Easter, he returned to Oxford to retake Responsions. But once in residence, he discovered that life at University College in 1916 was very different from his expectations. Out of a vast number of undergraduates only eight still remained. Part of the college had been given over for use as a military hospital, and even

Jack's rooms belonged to someone who was away at war.

Sadly, he failed the exam again. But happily, being in residence during the Trinity Term (summer) made him eligible to join the Officer Training Corps on the understanding he would continue his studies of maths and algebra.

In June, he was taken into the army. To his delight and astonishment he was stationed in Oxford at the new Keble College, but here, indeed, army training began. His room was a plain little cell; his hard, narrow bed devoid of either sheets or pillows. The only compensation was in having for his roommate a boy from Bristol, Edward Francis Courtenay Moore—otherwise known as "Paddy." He was the same age as Jack and very easy to get along with, even if he did seem rather immature for his age and rather too good to be human.

During the training period they underwent survival courses, such as camping in the Wytham Hills under severe conditions. On the first occasion it rained for days, and Jack wrote to Albert that he had already experienced life as it would be in Flanders' mud-filled trenches. Ironically, the training and harsh living conditions inspired his creative instincts and he was writing poetry in every spare moment. For the first time, he considered producing an anthology and approaching a publisher. In a letter to Arthur

Greeves, he jokingly remarked that if they were worthy of publication and if he didn't return from the war, there would at least be something of him left.

Weekends were free and on most of them he would return to University College for a good night's sleep in a proper bed before returning to Keble by 11 PM on Sundays. On these sojourns he explored parts of the College he would never have seen in peacetime. Eerily, deserted corridors echoed his footsteps as he trod through empty kitchens, utility rooms, tutors' chambers, dining halls, studies and lecture rooms, all shrouded in ghostly dust sheets. From grimy windows obscured by unpruned, neglected ivy clinging to the ancient walls, he would gaze out at the "dreaming spires and towers" and wonder if a time for idle dreaming would ever return. He could never have imagined loving a place so much. It even surpassed Little Lea in his affections.

Paddy Moore's widowed mother and his eleven-year-old sister, Maureen, had moved from Bristol to Oxford for a time to be close to him. And as his relationship with Jack gradually developed into friendship, he began taking him home on weekends along with some other young men. After a week of army privations, Jack reveled in the comfort, the meals and the pleasant company. He especially liked Paddy's mother, a warm, motherly woman of forty-five with a sense of humor to match his own. At the end of his three months' training he was given a month's leave. Two of the weeks were spent with the Moores in Oxford, the last two in Ireland.

By September, he was back in England, where, on the 25th, he was posted to Plymouth as a second lieutenant in the Third Battalion, Somerset Light Infantry. Within days of arriving there, on hearing he was being despatched to France and fearing they may never see each other again, he sent a telegram to his father:

HAVE ARRIVED BRISTOL ON 48 HOURS LEAVE. REPORT SOUTHAMPTON SATURDAY. CAN YOU COME BRISTOL? IF SO MEET AT STATION.

He was so obviously begging his father to come and see him before he left, and as Paddy's mother had now returned home to Bristol, he asked Albert to send his reply to her address. But when it arrived it read:

DON'T UNDERSTAND TELEGRAM. PLEASE WRITE.

Devastated by this blatant indifference, Jack sent another even more urgent message which Albert ignored completely.

Jack Lewis crossed the Channel and landed

in France on November 27, 1917. With three other newly commissioned young officers, he faced a fifteen-hour train journey to Rouen. It was a freezing cold night and one hour into the journey, as they passed through a tunnel, they heard a terrifying, crashing, grating sound which ended in the carriage door being wrenched from its hinges. With the train rocking and lurching, no one dared to move for fear of being thrown out through the gaping doorway. For hours, shivering and with teeth chattering, they sat perfectly still only to be rebuked the following morning by their commanding officer. Refusing to believe the door had fallen off of its own volition he accused them of vandalism.

On November 29, Jack's nineteenth birthday, he arrived at the trenches way up in the front line of the fighting. He knew immediately how wrong he had been in comparing the survival course on Wytham Hills with Flanders' mud. The reality was more like stepping straight into Hades—and he'd promised never to tread those dark ways again. Cold, slimy mud seeped into thigh boots through soles punctured when the wearer trod on pieces of jagged metal. Boots and unwashed clothes were worn for so long they stank and stuck to the body like a second skin. All day, shells blasted into the trenches at a rate of three every minute. Horribly wounded men crawled along like "half-crushed beetles." The dying and the dead were strewn all around him, some already in a state of decomposition. If his battalion was on the move, Jack often fell asleep and woke up again while marching.

Yet in the midst of such evils, contrary to what he had supposed, the appalling conditions brought out not the worst but the best in his fellow-men. It hadn't occurred to him from what diverse backgrounds his colleagues would hail. Along with the regulars, there were lawyers and farmers, butchers and poets, laborers and teachers, graduates and undergraduates, all totally out of their element. Some, like himself, were in command of older, experienced men. Jack felt that his only qualification for leadership was being in possession of a loud, booming voice. Ayres, his burly Canadian sergeant, took a fatherly interest in his young second lieutenant and, aware of his ignorance of warfare, advised him at every step.

And then there was Johnson. As a scholar from Queen's College, Oxford, he and Jack had much in common—but not everything. Johnson was a devout Christian whose sheer goodness and unquestionable faith in God disconcerted Jack. As if that wasn't enough, he also made him feel guilty to the point of hypocrisy because he never actually "got around" to admitting he was a non-believer. In Johnson, Jack thought he had acquired a life-long friend but, to his dismay, he was killed within weeks of their first meeting. But there were others around with the same high ideals and standards, and while Jack grudgingly resisted them, they annoyed him for clinging to an idiotic belief in Christ. How could these seemingly intelligent people be so misled? he asked himself.

At the beginning of February, he was "lucky" to fall ill with "trench fever" and be sent down the lines to a hospital and a welcome taste of civilization. The horrors of the past two months seemed so remote from clean laundry, vases of flowers and afternoon tea in the beautiful surroundings of a little fishing village that backed on to woods.

There was a limited choice of literature in the hospital, and one day Jack picked up a book by G. K. Chesterton of whom he'd never heard and soon found disturbing. Coupled with great humor, the author's goodness positively oozed from the pages, yet, once more, Jack found the man's faith in the Christian God irritating. Through that wretched war he had been introduced first to people like Johnson and now Chesterton. It appeared the trenches were as dangerous to atheists' peace of mind as they were to flesh and sanity.

His stay in the hospital lasted only a short while and he was back on the front line just days before the onset of the Battle of Arras, at Mount

Bernenchon. It was there that he experienced his sole wartime claim to glory. Looking out "over the top" one day, he nearly fell back into the trench with shock and fright to see, advancing on him, nearly one hundred German soldiers. Thinking his end was near, he closed his eyes waiting for the final blow but none came. Only when he looked again did he realize, they were all walking with arms upstretched in surrender.

Within a week of that episode, Sergeant Ayres was killed beside him, and Jack was wounded when fragments of shrapnel from an exploding shell were embedded in his arm and chest. Shock robbed him of his senses. He felt nothing. He couldn't breathe, and, believing he was dead, he lay perfectly still. Only his mind continued to function and his one regret was not having had time to complete his anthology before being shipped off to Hell. Now there would never be the time; neither would there be anything of him left on earth.

But then, slowly, pain began to seep through him until his body was completely enveloped by it—and he knew he was still very much alive.

9

... And Back

Jack regained consciousness in a military field hospital not far behind the lines. At first, his wounds didn't seem too serious but then complications set in. When an anxious-looking Warren arrived unexpectedly, although pleased to see him, Jack was alarmed—wondering if he'd been sent for because his brother was at death's door. But he was assured it was common practice for near kin to be allowed "up the lines" to see wounded relatives.

While he was in the field hospital, news came that Paddy Moore was missing. Shortly afterward, Jack was transferred back to "Blighty" as a stretcher case and taken to a hospital in London. When he saw other patients being visited by their families and friends, he sent letter after letter begging his father to come to see him.

However, Albert had no wish to disrupt his orderly life by sailing over to England to see his wounded son. In one letter, Jack wrote:

> Whenever I speak of you they all tease me and say they think my father is a myth of my imagination. No one believes that you exist!

Heartbroken, in another he wrote:

> Please come. I am terribly homesick and long to see you. That is the top and bottom of it.

Still, although Albert answered every letter, he made absolutely no reference to Jack's pleas.

As he improved, instead of being tormented by seeing others surrounded by their families, he took himself off to the nearby woods and countryside until visiting was over. There he would go over the manuscript for his anthology and write further poems, most of them inspired by his recent experiences in France. Soon the manuscript was ready for typing and then despatching to a publisher, and when this was done, he felt even more desolate and more keenly aware of his exclusion from the happy family groups around him.

Before leaving for France, Jack had promised Paddy that in the event of his not surviving the war, he would take care of his mother and Maureen. Now that he was getting better, he asked to be moved to Ashton Court, a Bristol hospital, at which he was closer to Mrs. Moore. There, he would be certain of at least one visitor. Anxious about her son, she too would be in need of consolation.

When Janey Moore visited the hospital, she told Jack that the other four boys who had spent weekends at Oxford with them had all been killed. Only Jack and her son remained. It was clear from that remark that she refused to believe Paddy was dead.

Only days later she received another telegram from the War Office confirming that her son was dead. To add to her sadness, on November 11, 1918, just weeks after news of his death, the war came to an end. Had it come sooner, he might have survived.

It was providential that Jack was in Bristol at that time. He had been in a light-hearted mood when he had given Paddy his promise to take care of his mother. Not for one second had it occurred to him that he would ever be expected to fulfill it. At eighteen, he'd believed himself and everyone else his age to be immortal. Now he knew better.

He was almost recovered by then, and had written to his father telling him that he hoped to spend Christmas in Ireland. Now, he was awaiting demobilization and wouldn't be able to go to Ireland until January, so instead he moved into the Moore's house. Placing Jack in the role of her lost son, Janey pampered him in a way he hadn't known since early childhood, and before long he was as fit and strong as ever.

Warren, home for Christmas, was very disappointed at hearing his brother wouldn't be there as he'd rarely seen him during the past two years. He was sitting in the study one day, remarking on this yet again to his father, when a cab drew up outside—and out stepped Jack. Having been declared "medically unfit" for the army, he'd been discharged immediately without waiting to be demobilized.

Albert was as unpredictable as ever. In spite of his heartless behavior toward "Jacko," he was so relieved at having his two sons survive the war, he forgot his usual frugality and opened expensive bottles of champagne in celebration.

January 1919 brought with it two pleasant and totally unexpected surprises for Jack. First, his anthology *Spirits in Bondage*, was accepted and the publishers wanted to see him in their London office. He could scarcely believe it when they told him the great John Galsworthy, while idly sifting through some papers on the publisher's desk, had come across Jack's manuscript and liked it. He particularly liked one poem, "Death in Battle," and wanted to include it in *Reveille*, a quarterly magazine he was producing for disabled ex-servicemen.

Back at Oxford in the same month, he came in for the second surprise. All ex-serving undergraduates were excused from taking Responsions. Granted this dispensation from the bane of his life—math and algebra—he was accepted as an undergraduate at University College, specializing in philosophy and ancient history. Particularly unpleasant was hearing how many of the undergraduates that he had known a year earlier were no longer alive. In that moment, winning the war seemed an extremely costly victory. And how very youthful the new freshmen appeared to be. "They look on us like old men," he wrote to Albert.

But among both new and old students, his greatest blow came from their attitude. Like Johnson, they were all exceptionally good and pure of mind. All believed in charity and public spiritedness to a degree that was unknown before the war. They also believed in sin, in souls and an afterlife. Even those who weren't already Christians, were heading in that direction.

In February, his poem "Death in Battle" appeared in *Reveille* along with contributions from such illustrious names as Graves, Belloc, Bridges and Sassoon. The following month, with the pseudonym of Clive Hamilton, his book *Spirits in Bondage* was published.

Jack was more pleased with the result than he'd anticipated and wrote to Albert hoping for some compliment. Perhaps pride in his son would stir him where compassion had failed.

The book caused no great stir among the literary critics but Jack didn't mind. What really mattered was that he was now an established writer. He had the rest of his life to produce more and better work.

Meanwhile, Mrs. Moore had decided to leave Bristol and move to Oxford where she could be with Jack, her adopted son. For the time being she and Maureen were living in rented rooms while they looked for a permanent residence there. This provided Jack with the home and family life he had longed for so desperately. Most days he went there for lunch, and spent every weekend with them.

Nicely settled in at college and with the publication of his book behind him, Jack got down to his serious studies. He loved Oxford more than ever—surrounded, as he was, by intelligent people all with the same interests as himself— well, almost.

No matter where he turned, his ungodliness was challenged, and again that feeling of guilt crept over him. It seemed there were more pitfalls for an atheist at Oxford in 1919 than he'd encountered from Johnson and his like in the trenches, or from Chesterton's book in the hospital.

At Easter, instead of going to Ireland, he went

to Bristol to help Mrs. Moore and Maureen with the packing and the move to their new home. When Albert heard of this he was furious and demanded to know why his son should choose their company in preference to his. He wrote to Warren complaining, demanding that he challenge his brother about his shabby treatment of his father.

But Warren remembered the time when Jack's very life was in imminent danger and he'd pleaded with his father to come to him only to be ignored. For a while, father and son stopped writing to each other, until Albert finally admitted to himself that he was at fault. He should have gone to Jack when he needed him.

When the summer holidays came around, Jack went home to Ireland but made it clear he wouldn't be staying for the full vacation—nor did he ever intend doing so again. It appeared that he had at last found his independence, and Albert had to accept it. If he objected to that arrangement, he feared Jack might not come at all. After his return to Oxford, letters started flowing between them again and their quarrel was over. It had taken a long time for Jack to take a stand, and he wished he'd done it sooner. He suddenly felt free of living under rule of someone's thumb—little realizing worse was to come.

To keep from dangerous Christian company, he befriended two confirmed non-believers,

Alfred Harwood and Arthur Barfield. Their personalities, interests and theories on everything were poles apart, with Jack somewhere in between. This promoted hours and hours of healthy argument from all three, and during the next two years they became almost inseparable. But eventually, even these trusted "friends" started questioning the source of life and the universe and Jack became thoroughly disillusioned. When they finally defected to Christianity, he was deeply offended not only by their ridiculous beliefs but by their attitudes. Just when they should appear tethered and under a heavy burden, they actually seemed liberated from some yoke.

In an effort to cool his relationship with Harwood and Barfield he found salvation in Neville Coghill. Now, here was a fellow who could be trusted not to fall foul of myths and legends. Neville was a good-looking, intelligent man; gallant and full of "old world charm," while having an impish sense of humor and a tendency to tease his friends. They met regularly in Jack's study or went for long walks around the town and out into the countryside talking about their studies, the books they were currently reading and everything else they had in common. It was on one of these treks when Christianity was lightly touched upon, and Jack scoffed at "those fools who rely on religion for moral support."

To Jack's amazement, instead of eagerly agreeing with him, his companion unashamedly announced that he was a Christian.

What was wrong with everybody? Jack wondered. Were they all going mad?

If he had encountered Hell in Flanders he was about to see another area of it in Oxford, for only weeks after questioning people's sanity, he actually witnessed that very torment.

Mrs. Moore's brother, whom everybody called "The Doc," was staying with her and unknown to anyone had been dabbling in the occult. At first, he appeared to be slightly depressed; then agitated. Later he became extremely emotionally disturbed and took to pacing the floor at night, refusing to go to bed. A wild look came into his eyes and he took on a totally different physical appearance that was frightening to see, especially for the small girl in the house. Eventually, even before the doctor's diagnosis, it was quite apparent he was completely mad.

Night and day, Jack took turns with other friends tending to the man's every need, which involved forcibly holding him down while he screamed and raged that demons were after him. This went on for two weeks until one night he let out an almighty inhuman howl that terrified everyone. As much for his family's peace of mind as for himself, he was rushed away to the hospital where, within hours of being admitted, he suffered a heart attack and died.

Only when his personal belongings were being sorted out and packed away was his involvement with the occult revealed. And how grateful Jack was for having discovered George MacDonald, whose fairy romance had brought him back from that very brink.

All the same, he wasn't going to be drawn into this other popular mythology, Christianity, even if it did have its roots in goodness. No, he must fight. He must. But what, he asked himself, was he fighting against? Why did he feel he was keeping *something* at bay?

To keep all his "treacherous" Christian colleagues away from him, he began staying alone in his study reading more than usual only to discover that his favorite authors—MacDonald, John Donne, Milton, Spencer and George Herbert—were all Christians.

In desperation, he turned to those he knew were securely atheist; H. G. Wells, George Bernard Shaw, Voltaire—and found them tiresome. It seemed there was no escape. Why did he feel like a hooked fish—struggling, yet slowly, inevitably being reeled in?

10

Under a Different Rule

*I*n 1922, at the age of twenty-four, Jack Lewis gained a first in philosophy and classics, yet failed to get a post at the University. He was offered one at Reading University about twenty miles away but was determined to stay at Oxford. After much consideration, coupled with advice from his tutors and his father, who offered to finance him for a fourth year, he agreed to stay on reading English Literature for a postgraduate degree.

His studies included learning the Anglo-Saxon language, which was reminiscent of those high-minded days of "Northerness" when a boy, and his yearning to learn Old Norse. But having long since abandoned the arrogance of youth, he was able to laugh, sometimes to be reduced to fits of giggles, at his own ineptitude when practicing the authentic guttural growls and throat-clicking sounds of the ancient tongue.

By now, those who had come to know Jack only since the war, really believed that Mrs. Moore was his mother. What is more, he never bothered to correct their assumptions, and if they ever wondered why her name wasn't Lewis nor his Moore he didn't bother to explain. It amused him to let them think that perhaps she'd been married twice and that Maureen was his half-sister.

What didn't amuse him, but he tolerated all the same, was the way Mrs. Moore was changing. He wasn't sure if it was a mother's normal reaction to losing her natural son or a resentment at him for usurping Paddy's place. Was it because they now had such a close relationship, one where "familiarity breeds contempt," he wondered. But no matter what the reason, she began to bully and order him about. When he was "home" for weekends or holidays, he found himself acting the role of domestic servant—dishwashing, preparing meals, cleaning grates, making fires and shopping.

Within his hearing, his "mother" often told visitors that Jack being there was like having another servant in the house. He was left with so little time for studying, he took to reading as he walked around. On evening walks through the woods, others would be startled when a resonant voice suddenly boomed out and Jack's great, lumbering figure appeared from amongst the trees. Book in hand and reciting notes, he would pass by completely oblivious of their presence.

While others thought he was under a family obligation, Warren knew the situation for what it was and couldn't understand why his brother put up with it. After all, he'd only promised Paddy to take care of his mother in respect to keeping in touch with her in case she ever needed help or advice. As it was, Jack had completely enslaved himself to her. He even wondered if, because their father had been such a strict disciplinarian throughout their childhood, Jack felt the need to always be controlled by someone. Had his experiences at Wynyard and the Coll conditioned him to a point where he was unable to function properly without the stress of oppression? Like Mrs. Moore, Warren, too, made scathing comments to friends that "After Jack has washed the dishes, if he's lucky, he may be allowed to go for a walk." Nonetheless, he decided not to interfere.

Warren was now stationed at Colchester, approximately seventy miles from Oxford, which was a lot closer than the brothers usually were. Some weekends Jack would escape from home and Mrs. Moore, take a train and join him there. They would spend the days riding out into the

countryside on Warren's long coveted motor-
cycle, and when they were together, all the years
that circumstances had kept them apart seemed
to melt away. On these occasions, even if they
were twenty-seven and thirty years of age, and
if Jack was a little heavier and they were both
losing their mops of brown hair, they felt like
small mischievous boys again. One time Jack
suggested driving into Wiltshire to take a look
at Wynyard, the old "prison camp," and Warren's doubts seemed confirmed. He never
wanted to see the place again, but had his
brother suffered so much at the hands of others,
he'd become insensitive to ill-treatment, and actually needed it?

Jack gained his Fellowship in 1924, and was
given a temporary post at University College
where he was giving four tutorials every day and
two lectures each week.

Always he lectured right up to the last second, collecting his books and papers and heading for the door while still talking. At other
times, he began his tutorial before reaching the
lecture room with students straining their ears
to avoid missing a single word as he marched
along the corridor towards them.

Even as a mature man, his clothes were still
ill-fitting—with oversized coats hanging from
his oversized frame. Out-of-doors, he invariably
wore a shapeless, slouch hat that had been

rained on more times than he could remember and sat on more often than that. The whole effect created a downright sinister impression, and although his students held him in the very highest esteem, they were often overawed by his appearance.

After a year in that post, in September 1925, Jack was offered a Fellowship at Magdalen College with accommodation in a beautiful suite of rooms and an annual salary of 500 pounds. The first was much appreciated; the latter essential, because what money hadn't gone toward his tuition and personal care had been used to support the Moores, and he was often penniless.

For the official welcome into Magdalen, Jack was required to kneel on a red velvet cushion while the vice president read a long speech in Latin before stepping forward to shake his hand saying, "I wish you joy." This was followed by his going around the room, shaking hands with all the other Fellows, who each echoed the vice president's words "I wish you joy."

How long it was, he thought, since he'd felt Joy with a capital J. Maybe now his lifelong ambitions were achieved, he would know it again—sometime in some way.

The first thing he did was to write and thank Albert for all his support over the years. For a man who was forever bemoaning his impending ruin, he had been extremely financially generous. Sadly, it seemed that was the only way in which he could show his affection. Albert was now sixty-two and old beyond his years. With the foibles and selfishness of age, he'd grown more difficult. But, with maturity, his sons had grown more tolerant and understanding toward him.

At Magdalen College, Jack's sitting-room overlooked sweeping parkland where deer roamed. It was his favorite season, with trees crimson in their autumn foliage, and with not so much as one gable of a building to be seen, it was difficult to remember he was in the center of the city. Alas, he wasn't permitted to spend as much time there as he would have liked.

Maureen Moore was now nineteen, and unlike Jack, she drove her own car, which gave her mother an advantage over him. Every day she insisted he come home for lunch at 1 PM and again at 4 o'clock for tea and, to ensure he obeyed, she sent Maureen to the college to collect him. The same procedure was followed every Friday afternoon, thus making certain that he also spent the weekends with her. All the time Jack was with Mrs. Moore he would, at her orders, be doing all sorts of menial tasks around the house, or sit listening to her as she talked incessantly about herself.

Weekdays however, he was required to sleep on campus and in the happy, peaceful college environment he found inspiration to write his epic poem "Drymer." Over the years, he had become an extremely observant person, noting the minutest detail of the most insignificant occurrence. He had acquired such mastery of words that even his description of a daily, mundane task, such as shaving, could be turned into an event of fascinating interest, and, upon publication, "Drymer" was highly acclaimed by the critics.

Jack's greatest friends at Magdalen were Charles Williams, who was writing *All Hallows' Eve*, and John Tolkien, who was planning a novel called *The Lord of the Rings*. His other close associates were William Yeats, Walter de la Mare and John Masefield, who was later to become England's poet laureate. At this time, Jack was beginning his first science fiction work, *Perelandra*. Because these young men were all writers and held regular discussions in Jack's rooms when they exchanged manuscripts for criticism and advice, they were known as "The Inklings." One of Jack's students was John Betjeman, also destined to become poet laureate, but who at that time was often reprimanded for his sloppy English and for not working hard enough.

In the midst of so much literary stimulation, Jack felt smugly secure from the threatening force of Christianity—until he came across what to him was a flaw in Tolkien's character. Not only was he a dedicated Christian, he was one of the worst kind—a Roman Catholic, with whom Jack had vowed *never* to associate.

After this discovery, he angrily paced up and down in exasperation. *Was there no escape from the wretched faith?* he demanded to know of his empty room.

It was one night when a friend, who was safely steeped in atheism, was sitting toasting his feet in front of a roaring fire in Jack's sitting-room, that he began to weaken—just a little. "It's a strange thing," said the friend, "this story about God. A very strange thing! You could almost believe what the Gospels say really did happen. Very strange, indeed!"

Jack stared at him in horror. If this man, who showed no fear of ever being converted, could actually sit there and make such arbitrary remarks, would it be safe to put his opinions to the test?

Delving into Norse, Greek and Celtic lore had done him no harm—well, not until he'd allowed them to drag him into their baser depths. Why not make a thorough examination of the universe and life? Was there a force—not one to do with a God, of course. But was there?

Jack felt he had been maneuvered into a long, narrow corridor from which the only escape was through a door at the far end—and he had the choice of either opening it or keeping it tightly shut. He preferred to keep it shut, but curiosity drove him to wonder what lay on the other side that so intrigued people whom he had hitherto believed bright and strong-willed.

11

Who Is Aslan?

Over and over Jack questioned, theorized and philosophized until finally, kicking and screaming in protest, he was dragged into submission. Somehow, it was reminiscent of being thrust into the black mourning suit for his mother's funeral. On this occasion though, he couldn't see that he was donning a shining, white mantle.

All Jack was prepared to admit was that there could possibly be a supreme power—but it wasn't a personal thing, not a God one could speak to, pray to. He didn't want to discover such a God anyway. He wanted to be his own master, free of obligation to any supreme being.

Always in pursuit of knowledge and having achieved some success in the Anglo-Saxon language, he embarked upon the daunting task of learning Old Icelandic. Perhaps it was a desperate effort to keep the now-accepted supreme power from encroaching on him any further. Maybe it was an attempt to feel again the elusive Joy he'd known during the Siegfried and Wagner period.

In the years since the war, his close friendship with Arthur Greeves had diminished. They met on holidays but rarely wrote letters. It was almost as if they had gradually outgrown each other and had little in common, but as Arthur was another dangerous companion—a Christian—Jack had every reason to avoid him. Now, with his resumed interest in Norse, Jack again began writing regularly to him, and with their renewed friendship, only then did Jack realize how much he'd missed his old confidant.

Jack had invented Animal Land at the age of five and perhaps a part of him had always lived there. In those early years, he had adored Beatrix Potter and fairy stories, but as he grew older he felt he ought to "put away childish things" and would have died of embarrassment rather than be caught reading such literature. Older still, and in his own words, he'd gained the confidence to "put away the fear of childishness and the desire to be grown up."

More and more, he turned to reading the simple stories of his childhood; of fairies, animals and imaginary lands. On his next holiday at Little Lea he recovered from the attic all the stories he and Warren had ever written and compiled them into an *Encyclopedia Boxon*.

The Christmas of 1927, to Mrs. Moore's chagrin, he spent in Ireland with his father, Warren and Arthur Greeves. They didn't know it was to be the last Christmas they would all be together. Even so, happiness mingled with sadness, because in January Warren was being posted to Shanghai in China.

Just a few weeks after Warren's departure for the East, his father, now sixty-four and retired, suddenly became ill with an incurable cancer. Jack was affected by this more than he would have ever imagined. Half term and Easter holidays saw him sailing over to Ireland to be with his father, most of the time sitting beside his bed just as Albert himself had done when Jack's mother was ill.

Complex as ever, Albert bore his painful illness with far greater courage than he'd shown when Flora was dying. He even showed more humor than at any of the better times in his life. During the summer holiday he was taken to the hospital, and in September, a matter of days before Jack was due back at Oxford, consultants decided that surgery was his only hope.

Although Albert didn't refer to it, Jack remembered his mother's unsuccessful operation for the same complaint. His one consolation was in reasoning that medical science had improved greatly over the past twenty-one years. But just as in Flora's case, for a while afterward it seemed he was recovering, then ten days later following a sudden relapse, Albert died.

In those days before flight was a normal means of transport, Warren was unable to get home to see his father in his final days nor could he be there for the funeral. Letters to and from Shanghai took six weeks to arrive, so although Jack had written to him every few days keeping him informed of their father's illness, he knew the letters weren't reaching him. This placed him in a terrible position, for it was he who had to send the telegram telling Warren of their father's death, and later compose a letter giving all the details.

In it, he referred to Albert as being someone who, though small in stature, could fill a room with his personality. He also remarked on how, now that their father was no longer there, he could do anything he liked in the house at any time—and it was hateful. Warren's tour of duty ended shortly afterward, and when he arrived home they faced the heartbreak of selling Little Lea.

Jack couldn't help wondering what had prompted him to learn the Icelandic language but he was thankful that he had, because but for that, he and Arthur Greeves might never have restored their friendship. Grandmother Hamilton, cousins Mary and Quartus and most of their other relatives were dead by this time; their younger cousins had long since married and left. Without "Norse" and Arthur, his father's death could have seen him sever all connections with Belfast.

During the breakup of the old family home, they came across legal and personal documents they never suspected existed—birth, marriage and death certificates dating back generations; diaries, photographs, letters and receipts. Later, Warren meticulously sorted and typed them all out; a work resulting in 3,300 single spaced pages revealed their entire family history.

When the brothers went up into the attic and looked around at their old toys and all the drawings of Boxon characters, they decided they held too many personal memories to be either left there, thrown away or given to others. And for two hardened materialists, they came to a strange decision. The only alternative, they decided, was to give them a decent burial. Together the brothers piled everything into open-topped tin boxes and carried them down to the garden where they dug a deep hole and buried them with much solemnity and emotion.

A few weeks after that painful episode, Jack was working in his study one evening when he suddenly became aware that his great battle was lost. *It* or *He* was right there in the room with him. He could *feel* goodness, love, light, warmth and hope all around him. Resignedly, yet purposefully, he slowly put down his pen, rose from his chair and knelt in prayer. At the age of thirty-one, after years of struggle against "the power," the dreaded "God" with his unavoidable net had finally closed in on him.

From that day, like all other converts he'd witnessed, Jack felt a lifting of some emotional weight. Even the loss of his father grew more tolerable as he accepted that death wasn't the end but merely the transition from this world to the next. Now he understood his deep involvement in *The Twilight of the Gods* and all things Norse. At his rejection of Christ, his mind had been cradled among the mythical gods while his soul matured for its return to the true faith. It was like having a physician advise a period of light meals until the patient is declared fit and ready to resume a normal diet.

When he realized the truth of what he had once done he couldn't—and never did—forgive himself for being confirmed and accepting communion as a foolish ritual. "Cowardice led me to hypocrisy. Hypocrisy led me to blasphemy" were his words.

All he wanted now was to help the atheists, skeptics, materialists and the so-called "freethinkers" to find the Lord for themselves. Just as when he had discovered Wagner, he knew the one way he could reach out to hundreds, thousands, or even millions of lost souls was through his writing. Christianity was introduced in his lectures, and the new-found faith of this once avowed non-believer was so sincere, so enthusiastic that he achieved the very effect he was aiming for. The doubters among his students began re-thinking and talking amongst themselves and his lectures were packed to standing-room only.

After the completion of the sale of Little Lea, Jack used his share of the money to buy a home for himself, his "mother" and Maureen. Situated in the beautiful Oxfordshire countryside and set in eight acres of lush gardens, The Kilns stood at the end of a narrow track. It had tennis courts, a swimming pool, and was almost surrounded by woods. With Tom the ginger cat, and the two dogs, Ricky and Mr. Papworth, they moved into the house in October 1930.

It is an odd fact that, at that particular period, when living in those idyllic, rustic surroundings, Jack turned to writing more science fiction with all its attendant dark and mysterious connotations. One was a novel, *Out of the Silent Planet*. The other was *The Pilgrim's Regress*.

Based on the same theme as that of Bunyan's *Pilgrim's Progress*, Jack's *Regress* was an account of his own conversion to Christianity.

That John Bunyan, charged with being an unlicensed preacher, was in prison when he began writing his book seemed to have evaded Jack. Maybe he ignored it because he was actually staying with Arthur in Ireland at the time of writing and the entire book was written in the matter of a few days. He returned to his personal prison later.

Warren was the most frequent visitor to The Kilns and was infuriated at the way Mrs. Moore treated Jack—and in his own home, the home he had made for her and her daughter.

As a boy and for his own reasons, Warren, like Jack, had also rejected Christianity. But as he grew older, and perhaps influenced by Jack, he turned once more to Christ. Now, while staying at The Kilns, whenever he and his brother set off for church and communion, Mrs. Moore yelled after them that they were "taking part in blood feasts."

When Warren retired from the army in 1932, he went to live with Jack and it seemed they had come full circle. Their lives began under the same roof, and as neither had married, they would now surely end together.

But their future was far from settled. Early in 1939, Jack began having terrible chest pains and often woke in the night finding difficulty in breathing. At first, it was thought he had a heart condition until X-rays showed a fragment of

First World War shrapnel that had been over-looked and was moving dangerously close to his lungs. An emergency operation was carried out and he was well on the road to recovery when, in September, war broke out again between Britain and Germany.

Although he was now forty-three and had been retired for seven years, Major Warren Hamilton Lewis was still "on reserve." And almost at once he was posted to a supply depot at Le Havre, a port in Northern France. Once more the brothers were separated, and as in the Great War, though Jack tried not to think about it, he was distraught with worry. On one occasion, while trying to prove just how *unconcerned* he was, Maureen noticed that the book he was "reading" was upside-down.

Recalling the horrors of the first war and having conceded that he wasn't alone in his anxiety, he prayed constantly for Warren's safety, even putting his feelings into verse.

> How can I ask thee Father to defend
> In peril of war my brother's head today?

Intent on making his own contribution to the war effort, Jack, in August 1940, joined the Home Guard. Donning khaki uniform and carrying a rifle, he reported for duty every Sunday, patrolling the University grounds with two other men from 1:30 AM until 4:30 AM.

By then he was a true champion of Christ and in that same year began his now famous radio broadcasts to the depressed nation, urging people to have faith and keep up their spirits.

He visited Army Units and RAF Stations offering comfort and strength to men about to face the enemy. Each day letters arrived from bereaved parents and widows saying how much he had helped them in their sorrow; helped them to trust in God just when their faith was in doubt.

He was writing books on religion and, recalling how Uncle Gussie used simple terms when talking to him, he determined that his books would hold no ponderous sermons or difficult-to-understand language. They were intended to reach people who read very little.

Soon his fame had spread around the world, and when people in America heard of the shortage of most commodities they started sending him food parcels.

As the war escalated and bombs rained down on London and some of Britain's industrial cities, parents sent their children away to the country, out of danger. Living in a huge house in the heart of rural England, Jack offered to take some of the evacuees. Three charming children arrived and, although accustomed to town living, to Jack's delight they loved animals and the countryside.

One thing he did find puzzling though, was that they kept asking him and Maureen "What can we do?" or, after having been offered a suggestion and carried it out, "What shall we do next?"

Such thoughts had never entered the heads of young Jack and Warren Lewis. There were always far too many things to do and never enough time in which to do them. From Maureen's attitude, it was evident she felt the same, although he never asked her about her early childhood with Paddy. Every day he racked his brains for ideas to keep the children amused and occupied, and then he hit on an idea that, if it worked, would benefit both them and himself.

Ever since his teenage years an idea for an animal story had been running around in his head but had never come to fruition. So far, all he had was the image of a faun with an umbrella walking through a snowy wood. That was as far as it ever got. On one occasion he had mentioned the theme and shown a few notes to John Tolkien, who thought it was a recipe for disaster. He hated everything about it to the point where he asked a mutual friend, "Does Jack know what he's talking about—a faun with an umbrella?"

Now with three, often bored children in the house and considering the circumstances under which they were there, he was reminded of it and began to write. But even as the story grew in length, he still didn't know where it would lead or even what its moral would be. Then, one day, quite unexpectedly he knew.

The wood was to be set in an imaginary country he called Narnia which could only be reached by passing through a—what? Ah, yes, a wardrobe. One of the main characters would be like Jack as he once was, misguided confused, searching and critical of those who didn't share his beliefs. Another character would have to be the "Great Knock." There would be the wicked Snow Queen, too, and—the story would ultimately lead its readers to the good Aslan. But who or what was Aslan? Jack knew *Aslan* was Turkish for "lion," but how did it manage to get itself into his story he wondered. Having ready-made critics under his roof, he tried the first chapter out on them and began:

This story is about four children whose names were Ann, Martin, Rose and Peter. But it is mostly about Peter who was the youngest. They all had to go away from London suddenly because of air raids and. . . .

12

The Final Joy

*I*n a contradictory fashion, God answered Jack's prayers for his brother's safety when Warren fell ill in France. It was a long and serious illness, but never at any time considered fatal. In 1941, after spending some months in a French hospital, he was invalided out of the army and sent home. Although the war continued for four more years, the personal involvement was over for the Lewis brothers.

Also in 1941, at the age of thirty-five, Jack's adopted sister Maureen married the musicmaster from Malvern College. This would seem to have lessened his domestic responsibilities but, on the contrary, they became more onerous.

At sixty-nine, Janey Moore was becoming impossible to live with. Totally self-centered, nothing and no one other than herself was of any consequence. She had a compulsion to quarrel with someone every day, usually with the servants—who left or were replaced at an embarrassing rate. Jack, of course, was always caught up in the middle of these scenes doing his utmost to keep the peace.

Books continued to pour from him and in 1942, he published *The Screwtape Letters*, which today would probably be described as black comedy. The main character, Screwtape, is an old devil who resides in a Hell run on the composite lines of a parliament, a prison, a secret service and a school. Again, although a work of pure fiction, as in *The Pilgrim's Regress*, it is based on Jack's personal experiences at various periods in his life. It turned out to be one of his best-known books and brought in more money than anything he'd written previously.

It was from this income that he was able to afford two servants, but with all the bad feeling between Janey and the staff, she suggested that they dispense with servants altogether and Jack could do the chores.

All of this he tolerated with saintly patience and good humor, while Warren was completely baffled that anyone would allow himself to be so abused. During the following four years, Janey's physical and mental health deteriorated. Warren felt slightly un-Christian at being secretly pleased when arthritis took the use of her legs and she could no longer manage to get downstairs.

It did not, however, stop her demands on Jack and now he was forever running up and down the stairs pandering to her every whim. Eventually in 1948, as she grew more and more senile in mind and body, she was taken into a nursing home. Jack visited her every single day for the final three years of her life.

Until then, Jack's books had been mostly for adults, but in 1950, the first of his Narnia stories, *The Lion, the Witch and the Wardrobe* was published. Ironically, Jack dedicated the book to his god-daughter, Lucy Barfield, whose father was Arthur Owen Barfield—that dangerous companion of his undergraduate days whom Jack had thought a traitor when he deserted materialism for Christ. Despite the book's popularity, it was ten years before he wrote a second Narnia story.

In January 1951, at the age of seventy-nine, Janey Moore died, and Jack was finally released from the promise he had made to his friend when he was a youth of eighteen. On that day, he had unknowingly committed himself to a life of verbal abuse and domestic drudgery that was to last for thirty-four years. It was a commitment that the materialistic Jack Lewis should have been able to relinquish at any time—and yet he'd chosen to honor it. And now, he wasn't sure if he felt freed from her tyranny or absolutely desolate at losing his "mother." Having his much-loved brother in the house was his solace.

In 1954, after twenty-nine years at Oxford, Jack became Professor of Medieval and Renaissance English at Cambridge University. He continued, however, to live at The Kilns in Oxford, spending only the obligatory weekdays at Cambridge.

It was around that time that he felt the urge to begin writing his autobiography, and looking back over his life, *Surprised by Joy* seemed an appropriate title. When it was published in 1956, his universal popularity soared to even greater heights. From all over the world he daily received letters; letters which often initiated new friendships. One of these was with a well-known poet writing under the name of Joy Davidman. He had met her a couple of years earlier when she was in England with her husband. Having just completed a book at that time about the Ten Commandments called *Smoke on the Mountain*, she had asked Jack if he would write the foreword.

Her real name was Joy Helen Gresham and she was an American Jew turned Christian. Her marriage had turned out to be disastrous and ended in divorce. At forty-one, she was left on her own to bring up her two young sons, twelve-year-old David Lindsay and Douglas Howard, age eleven. To escape the memories of her unhappy marriage, she had moved to England with her sons, who were now in a preparatory school at Oxford. On hearing of Jack's book, she wrote to congratulate him and so renewed their acquaintance.

Joy was not particularly "good-looking" but she was a wonderfully warm person. With the exception of Warren, she seemed to understand Jack more than anyone else—certainly more than any other woman, and their friendship developed into a great fondness.

Being the sole provider for her small sons caused Joy a lot of anxiety, because although she was a literary success, writing didn't bring the financial security she needed. Jack was aware of this and felt he had a ready-made solution. With his ever-increasing mountain of mail needing attention, plus his book manuscripts, lectures, radio talks and numerous newspaper and magazine articles always waiting to be typed, he asked if she would become his secretary.

This was precisely the work for which Joy was most suited, and so with her two boys and Snip her cat, she moved into The Kilns with Jack and Warren. It was a lovely home for David and Douglas, amid beautiful surroundings. They all got along well together—even the animals. They lived as one big family in a very happy household.

But no sooner were they settled, than Joy was

summoned to appear at the immigration office in London where she learned her permit to stay in England had been refused. She had no desire to return to America, nor could she afford to, and her children were happier than they had been in years. She was at her wit's end until Jack presented another solution.

Before discussing his idea with Warren, he thought deeply about it for days, wondering if it would work. Eventually, he told his brother what was on his mind and asked for his opinion. Warren reflected on the way their father had behaved towards Jack when Jack most needed him during the First World War. And yet Jack had spent every spare moment at his father's side when he was sick and dying. Warren grimaced at the memory of how Jack had voluntarily burdened himself for a large part of his life with the belligerent, ungrateful Janey Moore. Was it possible, Warren wondered, that his brother was only happy when bowed down with others' woes and responsibilities? Well, if that was what made Jack happy, Warren decided, it really had nothing to do with him and he told Jack so, adding that he'd better make up his mind quickly and not waste any more time.

So Jack asked Joy if she would marry him, because as his legal wife, she would be able to stay in England with her children. He explained that it would be merely a "marriage of convenience," neither would have any obligations to the other, and he would have his solicitor compile a marriage contract to that effect.

The ceremony was performed at the local Justice of the Peace, after which, spurning the traditional wedding festivities, they returned to The Kilns to get on with the day's work.

Within a few months of that loveless ceremony, Joy suddenly started suffering terrible aches and pains. At first, the doctors treated her for rheumatism, but instead of improving, she gradually got worse. With further tests they discovered she was seriously ill with bone cancer. There was no cure, no hope of a recovery.

Her condition deteriorated rapidly and she was soon admitted to the Wingfield Hospital at Oxford. Each time Jack and Warren saw her she was noticeably weaker, but always managed a smile for her visitors. It was when she was alone that the tears flowed, for worse than her impending death was the terrible thought of her sons being orphaned.

Jack prayed constantly for her. If there was no hope for her, then he prayed that the Lord would grant her a swift release from the terrible pain she suffered. At the same time, he prayed for her children, remembering what it was like to lose his own mother. In a sense he was pleased he had gone through that civil form of marriage with Joy because, although they had signed contracts relinquishing all obligation to each other, that union made him the boys' official step-father. Consequently, they were his legal heirs and they would always have a home and he would provide for them.

When he told her, Joy was so relieved that her sons would have a secure future that, despite her pain, she wept for happiness.

Now Jack was realizing that there was something more than compassion in his heart. Yes, he'd wanted to help Joy when she was in trouble with the authorities, and, yes, he wanted to help her sons when their mother died, but now, suddenly, without ever suspecting it, he realized that he loved her.

He had no idea how she would react to the fact, yet he felt compelled to tell her. Only then did she reveal that she loved him. Although their marriage had been an act of compassion on Jack's part, and of necessity on Joy's—they had since fallen very much in love.

With this, Jack again found himself proposing marriage—to the same woman and all within a matter of weeks. This time, though, it was going to be a Christian service filled with love—and sadness. That week, he wrote a woeful letter to Arthur Greeves saying he was about to become both a bridegroom and a widower within days.

The wedding was no occasion for rejoicing.

With the bride lying on her deathbed surrounded by flowers, the atmosphere was more akin to a funeral parlor with groom and guests feeling they were already in a state of mourning.

When Joy's death was drawing near, Jack brought her home. The hospital could do no more for her and she didn't want to die in the hospital. Now all he could do was sit beside her—as his father had with his mother, as he had with his father—until the end came. But Mrs. Joy Helen Lewis didn't die within a week or even a month of leaving the hospital. From the time she returned to The Kilns, she astounded her doctors when she gradually made what seemed a miraculous recovery.

Each day she gathered more and more strength, and after some tests and X-rays, the astounded doctors proclaimed Joy cured. They were utterly baffled as to how it had come about, but there were no signs whatever of any cancerous spots on her bones.

In only a short time, Joy was fully recuperated and she and Jack sat holding hands, praying together and thanking God for giving them a second chance.

At that particular time, Jack himself was undergoing tests for inflamed and painful joints, which sadly confirmed that he was suffering from a chronic bone disease. This made Joy and Jack determined to pack a whole lifetime into the short while they had left. The following year saw them visiting Ireland to see Jack's old home and to meet the few remaining relatives and friends he had there. Jack had never known such happiness and it seemed to him that the Lord was letting him make up for all the past miserable years of his life.

But before the holiday was ended, he began to feel ill and was forced to cut short their stay and return to England to consult his doctor again. The doctors thought it advisable for Joy to have a checkup, too, while she was there. To everyone's dismay, the tests proved that, although she felt fit and well, in truth she had simply been having a short remission. There were more cancerous spots on her bones; she was still terminally ill.

Now they were more determined than ever to live life to the full. Two years later, in April 1960, the two of them, as he said, "managed to *hobble* around Greece," which was an extremely adventurous undertaking for people in their state of health. For most of the time Joy was in a wheelchair, but they did succeed in struggling their way up to the Acropolis. But, whether it was from the heat, the exertion or simply that the end was near, Joy, during the holiday, gradually weakened again until at times she could barely stand up. To lend support, Jack would slip his arm about her waist, but being in poor shape himself it wasn't much help. Reluctantly, they decided to cut short their holiday and return home.

Suddenly on June 12, just four weeks after arriving back at The Kilns, Joy Helen Davidman Lewis died. Jack had few regrets. On the contrary, he had a lot for which to thank God. For a brief spell, he and the wife he never thought he would have, had known unbounded happiness together. That was more than either of them had ever hoped or prayed for.

With two adopted sons and the animals, plus Snip his step-cat, as he called him, Jack and Warren continued to live on at The Kilns just as they'd planned, ending their lives together as they began—under the same roof.

With the bone disease, Jack's health deteriorated rapidly. It was heartbreaking for Warren to see the brother, who always thought of himself as a "great, hulking, beefy lout," grow frail before his eyes.

On Friday, November 22, 1963, just six days before Jack's sixty-fifth birthday, Warren was reading his morning newspaper in the study when he heard a mighty crash upstairs. Now in his late sixties, he hurried to his brother's bedroom where he found him lying on the floor, his overturned chair beside him.

For Jack Lewis death had come swiftly, kindly and much sooner than expected, although he had been prepared for it for some time, and since discovering God, had harbored no fear of it. Like Barrie's Peter Pan, the little boy who never grew up, Jack had come to believe that "To die will be an awfully big adventure." It was—the final Joy.

Numerous books have been written about Clive Staples Lewis, Christian scholar, author, poet, broadcaster, lecturer and allegorist.

Many books were written *by* Clive (Jack) Lewis. Of those for adults, probably the best known are *The Screwtape Letters* and *The Allegory of Love*.

But of his books written for children, the sort he most liked to read, the ones he most liked to write, the best loved of all, are the Narnia stories which you must discover and read for yourselves—all of them.